Financial Controlling

Stefan Behringer

Financial Controlling

Springer

Stefan Behringer
IFZ Institut für Finanzdienstleistungen Zug
Hochschule Luzern
Rotkreuz, Switzerland

ISBN 978-3-658-40526-7 ISBN 978-3-658-40527-4 (eBook)
https://doi.org/10.1007/978-3-658-40527-4

Responsible Editor: Vivien Bender
This Springer imprint is published by the registered company Springer Fachmedien Wiesbaden GmbH, part of Springer Nature.
The registered company address is: Abraham-Lincoln-Str. 46, 65189 Wiesbaden, Germany

Preface

Financial Controlling is a support and basic function of every management. In most companies, all employees are either direct addressees of controlling and use the information provided there, or they are at least indirectly affected because decisions are made on the basis of controlling reports. For these reasons, financial controlling is a mandatory part of almost all business-oriented bachelor's and master's programs.

The present textbook is intended to provide basic knowledge of financial controlling. The tasks of controlling will be presented first. This will compare what controllers do in practice and what they should do according to the ideas of business theory. In ▶ Chap. 1 it will also be discussed how financial controlling can be organized in companies.

▶ Chapter 2 deals with the information provided by financial controlling. Internal and external accounting form the information basis. The chapter on the information function shows how the numbers from these accounting systems are processed into key figures and processed in cost management instruments. While ▶ Chap. 2 deals with the past-oriented preparation of information, ▶ Chap. 3 the future-oriented tasks of controlling are represented by planning. It is discussed how a planning process works, which functions it should fulfill and what contribution planning can make to the achievement of corporate goals. A key focus of this chapter is also which goals a company can reasonably pursue. Furthermore, potential problems of planning and possible alternatives are presented.

▶ Chapter 4 summarizes the past- and future-oriented perspectives. The target value (the plan value) is compared to the actual value. This chapter presents the possible interpretations of deviations between target and actual.

▶ Chapter 5 deals with the digitalization of financial controlling and the controlling of digitalized companies. This addresses a current development that is becoming increasingly established in the everyday life of many companies. In the previous edition, this area was still presented in the trends, as many things were not foreseeable. Now we can assume a lot more knowledge about digitalization and artificial intelligence to be certain. Risk management and compliance remain trends (▶ Chap. 6). Sustainability, which also plays a role in controlling, is becoming increasingly important—forced by regulations at national and European level in particular. This is addressed in ▶ Chap. 6.

The aim of this textbook is to present the activities of financial controlling and to give an insight into basic instruments of controlling. This gives interested parties an initial insight into an activity in controlling. Addressees of controlling information receive the necessary tools to interpret the information. In addition to the German perspective, this book also takes into account the situation in Switzerland at many points.

The book is aimed at students of business administration and other business-oriented courses. Many examples and case studies help to illustrate the material presented. At the end of each chapter there is a short summary that brings the essential statements to the point. The learned content can be checked with the help of short tasks (Let's check). Connecting tasks also give impulses for further thinking and deepening of the learned content. The solutions to all tasks of the book can be obtained via the SN Flashcard App of Springer-Verlag.

I would like to thank all those who have contributed to the success of this book, in particular all those involved at Springer-Verlag and the team at IFZ Institut für Finanzdienstleistungen Zug at the Hochschule Luzern.

Stefan Behringer
Rotkreuz
November 2020

Contents

Abbreviations

Fig.	Figure
Para.	Paragraph
AktG	Stock Corporation Act
BilMoG	BilMoG
CAPM	Capital Asset Pricing Model
DIH	Days Inventory Held
DSO	Days Sales Outstanding
EBIT	Earnings before Interest and Taxes
EBITA	Earnings before Interest, Taxes and Amortisation
EBITDA	Earnings before Interest, Taxes, Depreciation and Amortisation
EBT	Earnings before Taxes
FCF	Free Cashflow
GmbH	Gesellschaft mit beschränkter Haftung
HGB	Handelsgesetzbuch (German Commercial Code)
IAS	International Accounting Standard
ICV	International Controller Association
IFRS	International Financial Reporting Standards
InsO	(German) Insolvency Code
IT	Information Technology
AI	Artificial Intelligence
KontraG	(german) Act on the Control and Transparency of Enterprises
lmi	performance-related process
lmn	performance-neutral process
RoCE	Return on Capital Employed
RoI	Return on Investment
RPA	Robot Process Automation
SMART	Specific, Measurable, Accepted, Realistic, Time bound
VUCA	Volatility, Uncertainty, Complexity, Ambiguity
WACC	Weighted Average Cost of Capital
WHU	Wissenschaftliche Hochschule für Unternehmensführung

Basics of Financial Controlling

Contents

S. Behringer, *Financial Controlling*,
https://doi.org/10.1007/978-3-658-40527-4_1

1

Learning Agenda

Controlling is a multi-layered concept. With controlling, designated institutions carry out very different activities and assume different roles in companies. The basic part of this book approaches the field from both practice and theory. The theoretical guiding principle of "securing rationality of leadership" encompasses the previously presented practical fields of application of controllers. Subsequently, the possibilities of organizational placement of the controlling department as a staff or line department together with the hierarchical placement in the company organization will be discussed. In large companies, the question also arises as to whether controlling should be organized centrally or decentralized. This is associated with various advantages or disadvantages for the perception of the securing of rationality of leadership as the core task of controlling. In addition, the chapter deals with the professional and interdisciplinary requirements that successful controllers should meet.

Basics of Controlling		
Tasks of controllers in practice	What tasks do controllers take on in practice? What different roles can controllers play in practice?	▶ Sect. 1.1
Theoretically derived tasks of controlling	What theoretical justification is there for the establishment of controlling departments in companies?	▶ Sect. 1.2
Organization of controlling	What alternative organizational structures are there and what advantages and disadvantages are associated with them? How can controlling be organized in large companies with several business units?	▶ Sect. 1.3
Profile of requirements for controllers	What professional and cross-professional qualifications should a successful controller have?	▶ Sect. 1.4

1.1 Tasks of Controllers in Practice

If you tell your friends about your work in controlling, it seems that at least one aspect of the work is clear to everyone: A controller controls. The linguistic proximity of controlling and control suggests this, but this is a misunderstanding. The English verb “to control” has the meaning of “steering” in particular. This corresponds more to the self-image of the controller.

In a nutshell: Controllers are concerned with corporate governance. Control is part of it, but by no means the most important or even the only one.

In practice, the activities of controllers are very different. The tasks range from accounting to top management consulting with a strong factual influence on corporate management. The International Controller Association (ICV), in which controllers from different European countries have joined forces, understands the controller as a management partner. In its mission statement it says (ICV 2013):

> Controllers contribute as partners of management to the sustainable success of the organization.
> Controllers …
>
> 1. shape and accompany the management process of target setting, planning and control, so that every decision maker acts in a target-oriented manner.
> 2. ensure the conscious engagement with the future and thus enable opportunities to be seized and risks to be managed.
> 3. integrate the goals and plans of all stakeholders into a coordinated whole.
> 4. develop and maintain the controlling systems. They ensure data quality and provide decision-relevant information.
> 5. are committed to the welfare of the organization as a whole as the business conscience.

With this guideline, the profession of controllers takes on the concept of **business partnering**. Even though controllers have always served as advisers to management, the role of business partner is more comprehensive. The controller supports the executive management. He is not only an expert in his actual field, accounting. He also knows the peculiarities of the industry and can express himself competently on business issues. Here, the misunderstanding mentioned above of translating controlling with control can be hindering. Often the middle management has difficulties with controllers. Therefore, a clear definition of roles and description of tasks of controlling is extremely important. Because even too much partnership can damage the (still to be defined) tasks of controlling: control is one aspect of controlling. Those who are controlled are not usually made into trustworthy partners.

In practice, controllers fulfill many different tasks. The controller panel of the WHU Koblenz regularly surveys controllers about their tasks. ◘ Table 1.1 shows the time requirements of controllers for individual tasks. In 2014, the participants were asked how much time they spent on specific tasks. According to this, controllers use the most time (27% of their total budget) for tasks in corporate planning (budget, medium-term and strategic planning). The provision of information to management (reporting) follows with 21% of the total working time. This is followed by project work and other advice to management.

Many of these tasks do not fit directly into the business partner role as propagated by the ICV. Reporting, cost accounting and large parts of the planning tasks are not compatible with the close partnership with decision-makers. However, these tasks are a necessary prerequisite for qualified management consulting. These rather technically oriented, dry activities often still shape the everyday life of controllers. In practice, the controller is therefore often still the bean counter, which has shaped the image of this activity for a long time. However, a large part of these activities is now automated. This also represents a danger for the future role of controlling in companies. The management can retrieve the information itself from the IT systems. A mediator is no longer necessary. Complex preparations are carried out by new professions such as the data analyst or data scientist. Here, less business-related than technical and mathematical-statistical expertise is

◘ **Table 1.1** Tasks of controlling: Time requirements for individual tasks in % of the total time budget

Reporting	21%
Project work	16%
Other management consulting	15%
Budget planning and control	14%
Cost accounting	8%
Medium-term planning and control	7%
Strategic planning and control	6%
Investment planning and control	5%
Other	8%

Evaluation from the WHU Controller-Panel (► http://www.whu-on-controlling.com/zahlen/. Accessed on 04.05.2017)

required (Ulrich and Stier 2020). Here the controller has to defend his role with business-related expertise.

The actual role taken on often depends on the company's situation and culture. The roles can be differentiated according to the company's culture (Lambert and Sponem 2012):

- In companies operating in growth markets, controllers are rarely involved in strategic decisions. They are active in the fields of reporting and budgeting and control. Management sees them as necessary, but their role is that of an inconspicuous service provider.
- In companies dominated by marketing or technology, controlling plays a significant role for central management. Controlling is the management's representative and ensures its decisions through control. However, controlling is not itself involved in the decision-making process on the strategic situation.
- If the marketing and financial perspective are equally strong in companies, controlling can actually play the role of business partner. In these companies, management decisions are prepared in detail—also because there are two different, equally powerful centers of power. Here, controlling is of paramount importance. However, controlling is faced with the dilemma of "involvement vs. independence": If it is involved in decisions, as is often the case in these companies, it can no longer assess them impartially ex post (Hopper 1980).
- Controllers in companies that have run into financial difficulties can become omnipotent. Costs and efficiency are of paramount importance, controllers also become very important. Formally, controllers release decisions through their evaluations and de facto receive a stronger position than operational management. They are no longer business partners but become decision-makers themselves.

> In a nutshell: The role that controlling plays is strongly dependent on the company culture and the financial situation of the company. In companies with a strong marketing or technology focus, the influence of controlling is below average while it is above average where there are financial difficulties. They are only business partners in companies where there is a balanced distribution of power between the individual departments.

In many companies, what distinguishes the controller in particular is his competence in obtaining, processing and selecting target-oriented information. To what extent the controller is involved in further processing the information and the associated decision-making process depends on the actually lived role in the company.

In smaller companies, controllers (or employees who are responsible for controlling tasks in addition to other areas) take on more operational tasks from the areas of planning, reporting or cost accounting (Becker et al. 2016a). In larger companies, in addition to the classical, more financially oriented controlling, there are often a number of **specialized controlling departments** that deal with special controlling issues from their specialist areas: IT controlling, logistics controlling, personnel controlling, marketing controlling. In addition, there are some industries that also require special controlling due to their special features. These include, for example, banks, insurance companies, hospitals but also public companies, universities or research institutes.

1.2 Theory-Based Derivation of the Tasks of Controlling

The management of a company has to make a variety of decisions: Should we invest in a new plant? Should the new product be launched first in Europe or in America? Should a new employee be hired or the branch be closed in a foreign city? From a business point of view, a decision-making process that is strictly based on the **purpose-means rationality** would be correct: The resources used to achieve a goal must be **effective** and **efficient**. "Effective" means that they are suitable for achieving the set goal. "Efficient" means that there is a reasonable relationship between resources used and goal achievement. If a small fire is extinguished with champagne, this is effective. It is only efficient if no other suitable liquid was available.

> In a nutshell: Controlling supports the management of the company in complying with the purpose-means rationality, that is, in the efficient and effective use of resources to achieve the set goals.

Plans play a key role in achieving the means-ends rationality. Plans take future "action thinking […] action handling" in advance (Kosiol 1967, p. 79). During the planning process, it is thought through which activities the company would like to carry out in the next planning period. Furthermore, during the planning process, it is considered which sequences of actions will result from these activities. This gives the actors concrete goals that are then also the basis for control activities. Since they set goals, they are constitutive for the assessment of the achievement of means-ends rationality. The creation and processing of plans thus makes a important contribution to ensuring the greatest possible rationality. In addition, the probability of success of the company is improved by a better allocation of resources. The various planned activities of the company are coordinated with each other. This makes it possible to have a coordinated approach within the company, which improves the probability of success. Planning is therefore a prerequisite for a targeted control of the company.

Of course, controllers also have no certain view of the future. Which boundary conditions (reactions of employees or competitors) actually occur is completely open. Full foresight—a prerequisite for rational action—is not given in reality. All people, and thus the real manager and his controller, act only in the state of limited rationality (**bounded rationality,** Simon 1961). The manager is indeed willing to make a rational decision, but due to the limitations of human perception and information processing, he is actually not in a position to make rational decisions at all times. If you compare the assets of humans with the requirements for rational action, the limitations become apparent. These limitations are particularly expressed in (Sanders and Kianty 2006, pp. 171 f.):

- **Limitations of knowledge:** There is not complete information available about all conceivable states of the company and the market. The manager does not know what the competition is planning or which potentials are still dormant in the company, e.g. which employees have special talents. Managers also do not know which products will be conceivable in the future, etc. They simply do not know all the possibilities that are actually open to them. The human brain is not designed to know everything (and to relate all pieces of knowledge to each other). This means that an essential requirement of the theoretical model of homo oeconomicus—the fundamental assumption of behavior of economics, which allows knowledge in spite of the complexity of reality at all (Stadermann 1987, p. 16)—is not fulfilled and thus rational action in the sense of this model is practically not possible.
- **Limitations of anticipation:** The possible consequences of actions are not fully foreseeable. If the manager decides on a price reduction, he does not know how consumers and competitors will react to this price reduction. Also the reaction of employees, who are considered to be particularly talented, to the closure of a branch is not predictable. In view of the unpredictability of the future, decisions are necessarily made on the basis of incomplete information.

- **Limitations of action possibilities:** The management is not fully aware of which action possibilities are available. On the one hand, only the possibilities that are known today are perceptible. New possibilities that would simply result from waiting, e.g. through the further development of a technology, are unknown. But due to the limited processing capacity of humans, even today's actually available possibilities are not fully known. At this point, the limitations of action possibilities and knowledge overlap.

> In a nutshell: Entrepreneurial decisions are made in the state of limited rationality. It is the task of controlling to show rationality deficits and to sensitize the management.

The limitations of limited rationality lead to the fact that the management of a company cannot make decisions with complete information. But this is precisely the assumption made by economic models in most cases. If one adds that the management everyday life is strongly characterized by interruptions and a manager extremely rarely has the opportunity to deal intensively with a question (Mintzberg 2009), the limits of rational decision-making become clear. However, since it is the aim of every company to make decisions as rational as possible, a function is created in the company with the controlling, which explicitly gets the task to ensure the rationality of the management decisions as far as possible. This task of the controlling is referred to as the **rationality assurance of leadership** (Weber and Schäffer 1999).

Controlling actually takes on the tasks for rationality assurance. Thus, plans—as shown—are constitutive for rationality compliance because goals are specified in a binding manner through them. Reporting and other activities of information provision also contribute to rationality assurance, since only relevant information can be used to make management decisions on the basis of an adequate level of knowledge, which is a prerequisite for rational decisions. Support of management can also be subsumed under the term rationality assurance. On the one hand, controllers take on tasks to relieve management. These are mostly decision-making activities, such as investment accounting, planning, etc. Here, controllers have specialization advantages because they carry out these activities more often. This relieves managers of their scarce time budget. They have time to take care of other important, non-delegable activities. On the other hand, controllers advise management. This allows management decisions to be considered from a second perspective. Controllers take an independent look at decisions. This can ensure that managers make their decisions more objectively and not just in their own interests. The structure of this book follows the tasks of controlling (see ◘ Fig. 1.1): ▸ Chap. 2 deals with the information function, ▸ Chap. 3 explains the steering function, which is understood to mean planning in particular, and ▸ Chap. 4 the control function. All of these are sub-areas of the rationality assurance function, which is the overall goal of controlling.

It is often objected in criticism of the rationality assurance function that the tasks of controlling are drawn too far, since the controller is also a person who is concerned with his own advantage and only equipped with limited rationality (e.g. Horváth 2002, p. 341). Of course, these observations are justified. Controllers are also "only" human beings for whom limited rationality applies. Despite the obvious shortcomings of the people who work in controlling, the goal of better decision-making speaks in favor of setting up a function that feels committed to the guideline of rationality assurance.

The description of the rationality assurance tasks of management also immediately results in the delimitation between the tasks of controlling and management. The managers are responsible for the management of the company. They therefore have to make the decisions and are responsible for the consequences that arise from a decision. The controller is an advisor who prepares the decisions but does not make them himself. Here one can use the image of the driver and the passenger. The manager is the driver who holds the steering wheel in his own hand and decides which way is actually driven. The controller is the passenger who reads the map and prepares the manager's decisions with his suggestions for a route.

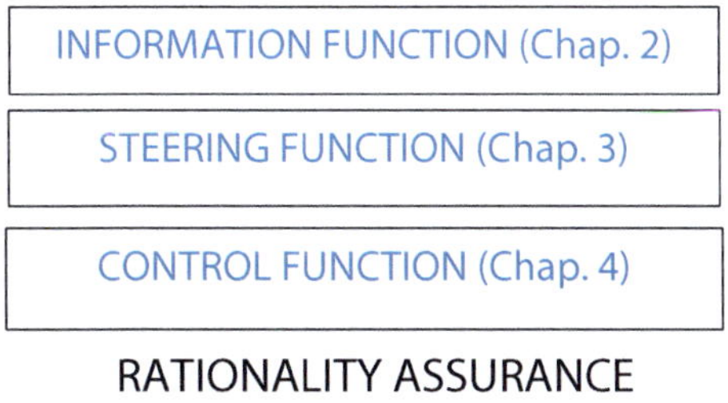

◘ **Fig. 1.1** Functions of controlling and chapters of this book

1.3 Organization of Controlling

1.3.1 Controlling as a Line or Administrative Department

In the previous sections, the tasks of controlling have been derived empirically and theoretically. Now the question arises as to who should be the bearer of this task (controlling) and how this task should be organized.

There are independent controller positions in almost all large companies. The size of the company and the size of the controlling department are directly related to each other: The larger the company, the larger the controlling department is usually. This is plausible because coordination is more difficult in a larger organization and plans and reports gain in importance as coordination instruments.

It is often discussed whether controlling is a line or a staff function. **Line functions** have disciplinary authority, they lead and make decisions to which others are bound. Controllers are then on an equal footing with other departments in the line (e.g. production, sales). **Administrative positions** only take on indirect management functions. They advise, analyze and prepare decisions. They have professional authority, but do not decide themselves. However, these departments often have a high degree of informal power due to their direct access to corporate management. Their advice is heard and often implemented, even if they do not have the formal authority to make decisions.

Controllers are often organized in classical administrative departments. They support the leadership and usually do not decide for themselves. Controllers only have decision-making competence for their own affairs. This includes, for example, the sequence and premises of planning, their own personnel selection and workflows. In addition, they are only active in an advisory and questioning capacity. For planning, this means that the controller questions the content but is not authorized to make decisions on the content of the plan himself. However, with the decision-making competence over the planning process, the purely decision-making preparatory role is already exceeded. Especially the coordination of other areas requires that a partial line responsibility in controlling is necessary. If, for example, controlling recognizes that the partial plans of the departments do not fit together (e.g. marketing plans a campaign for a product for which production is reducing capacity), it must name and intervene. An administrative department communicates this discrepancy to the management, which then commissions the two involved departments to coordinate properly. How-

Table 1.2 Advantages and disadvantages of the administrative and line organization of controlling

Controlling as a central department		Controlling as a line department	
Advantages	**Disadvantages**	**Advantages**	**Disadvantages**
High neutrality Inclusion in the flow of information and close contact with the management	No authority Possibly low authority	Authority High importance and authority in the organization	Possibly poor integration into decisions

Deimel et al. 2013, p. 39

ever, in many companies this process is abbreviated: Controlling orders both departments to clarify the matter. For this reason, in most companies controlling is formally carried out as an administrative department, but de facto they have significantly more power and competence, some of which are borrowed from the line organization.

The **informal power** that controllers exert arises directly from their direct access to management. If controlling prepares decision-making bases, the selection and presentation of information often determines the decision made at least to a significant extent. On the other hand, it would be wrong to formally attribute to controlling all the powers of direction they have informally. In many companies this would mean that the company would actually be controlled by controllers. ◘ Table 1.2 summarizes the advantages and disadvantages of the administrative and line organization of controlling.

1.3.2 Hierarchical Classification of Financial Controlling

Financial controlling receives the highest possible authority when it is anchored directly in the management or the board, as shown in ◘ Fig. 1.2. This automatically gives the controlling instructions rights that facilitate the coordination of the individual areas and thus reduce the discussed problems for line and administrative departments. The controller is in this case an equal member of the management. In order to be able to carry out the role of rationality assurance of the management in an appropriate way, a comprehensive information supply is necessary. The controller can only

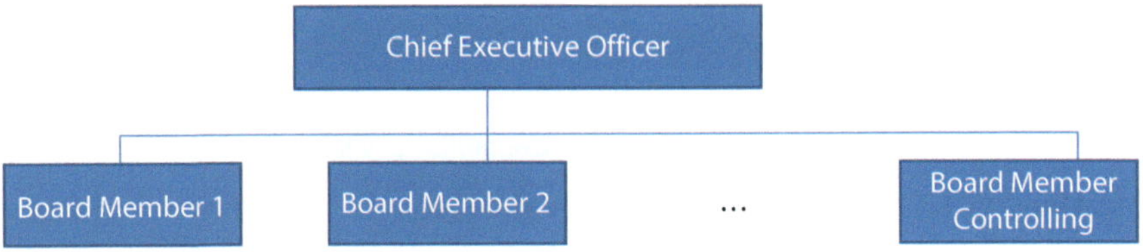

Fig. 1.2 Organization of controlling at board level

provide relevant information if he knows about decisions. With the location of controlling in the top management this would be secured. However, the problem with this high hierarchical classification is that the controller himself becomes part of the top decision-making body and thus loses his independence. This could at least make it more difficult to critically question, as it belongs to the rationality assurance of the management. In addition, controlling is not completely relieved of the management in this case. Can coordination problems otherwise be discussed on a lower level with the controlling as a moderator, these tasks land again in the overall board.

More often encountered in practice is the anchoring of the controller on the second line level. Then the head of controlling reports to a managing director "finance" or "accounting" (CFO), as shown in Fig. 1.3. The hierarchical ordering is still outstanding, but the controller can maintain his independence and is not himself part of the decision-making bodies. However, the acceptance by other departments is no longer self-evident. The acceptance must be earned through value-added work, otherwise the controlling is left behind by other functional areas and is particularly excluded from the informal flow of information.

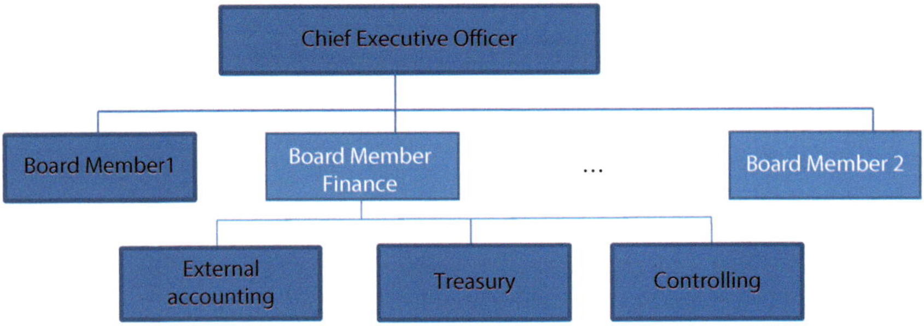

Fig. 1.3 Organization of controlling at the second hierarchical level

> In a nutshell: The hierarchical ordering of financial controlling is in the tension field between proximity to decisions and information on the one hand and the independence of controlling on the other. Many companies solve this dilemma by locating controlling on the second hierarchical level.

If controlling is located even lower in the hierarchy, there is a lack of decision-making competence and access to the decision-making bodies. Therefore, this ordering is mostly only found in companies in which financial controlling plays a subordinate role (e.g. growth companies or marketing or technology-driven companies).

1.3.3 Central or Decentralised Organisation of Controlling

In larger companies or groups, the question also arises as to whether controlling should be centrally or decentralised. If controlling is centrally organised, there is a controlling department which is located at corporate level, while in decentralised organisation there are several controller positions distributed across the organisation in the various business areas.

In the **central** organizational form (cf. Fig. 1.4) the controlling department provides support for both the management to which it is directly subordinate and the decentralized business units. In this constellation, controlling is directly linked to the management and thus involved in all essential decision-making processes. In addition, this can ensure that standards (e.g. definition of key figures) are applied uniformly throughout the

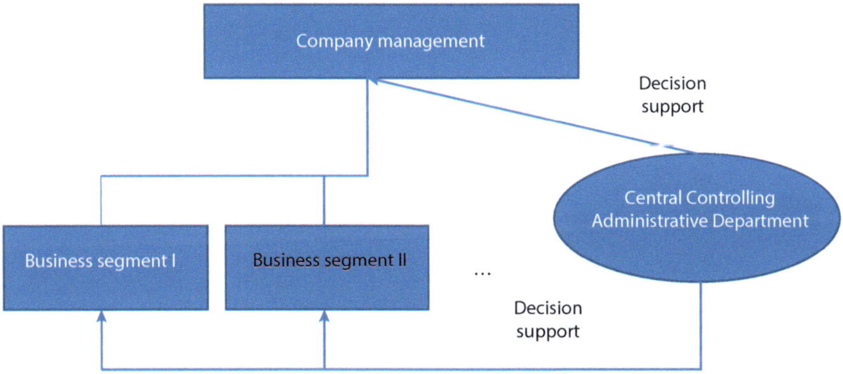

Fig. 1.4 Central controlling organization

1

company. However, the sometimes low acceptance in the business units is problematic. The central controller can be misunderstood as the controller of the management, which makes his role as an internal consultant more difficult. If the different business units require different approaches, a formal equal treatment (with the same key figures) but an unequal treatment in content (by the same interpretation of different situations) can result.

In a **decentralized controlling,** each business unit has its own controlling department. This constellation is schematically shown in ◻ Fig. 1.5. The controlling departments are largely autonomous and determine for themselves how they proceed. Their first loyalty is to their business unit, which makes it difficult for the management to receive independent information. Here they are also fully involved. A critical point is that difficult decisions (e.g. the closure of an area) are rarely proposed by the controlling function in this constellation. The financial controlling lacks critical distance to its business unit. Furthermore, it is not guaranteed that standards and methods are applied uniformly. In many cases, this model also leads to an increased need for personnel in corporate controlling, as replacement rules must be introduced for each area.

> In short: In the central organizational form, the controlling reports professionally and disciplinary to the management. In the decentralized organizational form, the controlling reports professionally and disciplinary to the heads of the business units.

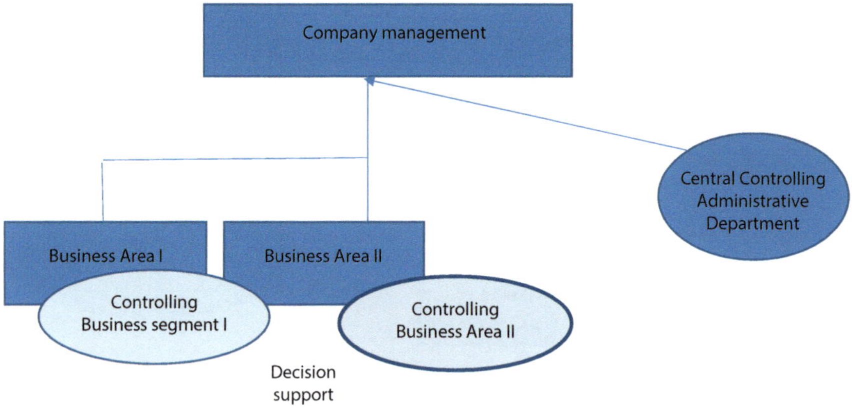

◻ **Fig. 1.5** Decentralized controlling organization

In order to be able to use the advantages of both organizational forms, many companies work with a mixed central-decentral structure. In this case, the controlling areas receive two superiors. The central controlling department is the professional superior, the disciplinary superior is the specialist department. This compensates for two disadvantages of pure decentralization: methods can be applied uniformly and the information flows to the management, as the central corporate controlling has full access to the findings of the decentralized controllers. Nevertheless, the heads of the business units still receive confidential advice, as the controllers report disciplinary to the heads of the business units.

The logical assignment requires that operational tasks be located in decentralized controlling, while strategic tasks that concern the entire company are carried out centrally. In reporting, one should realize as much centralization as necessary, but allow as much decentralization as possible. Decentralization leads to a better understanding of the reasons for certain business developments. Recognizing risks is much easier for employees who are closely related to the business than for the central department. Therefore, business-related tasks should ideally be given to the operational, decentralized controlling unit, while the central controlling unit must be powerful enough to ensure the reporting of difficult situations and to ensure that methods are applied uniformly. This is important because, by definition, controlling is also a rationality safeguard for corporate management and therefore has a special meaning for corporate management.

In a corporation, the organization of controlling must take into account an additional level of complexity. A corporation consists of at least two legally independent companies, one of which controls the other. Important business matters are linked to the legal entity (e.g. insolvency, taxation, reported profit). But economically, the corporate construct can be important (e.g. in planning). In addition, the group result is added to the result on the single company level. This results in two levels for controlling: Decentralized controlling is located in the subsidiary companies while group-relevant issues including a view of the subsidiary company as a whole are located in group or holding controlling at the group level (Behringer 2018).

▶ Example: Cooperation of central and decentralized controlling in the VW Group

In addition to a controlling department that is located at the group board of directors for finance, there is also a controlling department in all subgroups (e.g. Audi, Skoda, Seat), which is also located at the respective finance director of

1

the subgroup. Central group controlling is responsible for overall steering and coordination in the group as a whole. The controlling departments in the subgroups, on the other hand, deal with more operational issues: There are special controlling departments (e.g. for the group brand Volkswagen) for production, procurement, sales or logistics. In order to ensure uniformity, central controlling and controlling departments of the subgroups coordinate and work together on an equal footing (Britzelmaier 2013). ◄

1.4 Profile of Requirements for Controllers

The diverse tasks that controllers have to perform in practice and the high importance they have for successful corporate management require them to have diverse professional and interdisciplinary qualifications. In particular, knowledge of accounting, which is the basis of controlling activities, and knowledge of the common controlling instruments are to be mentioned as necessary requirements. No reporting in companies is imaginable without the use of modern IT. Together with the penetration of IT applications, IT skills have become increasingly important for controllers. This trend will continue. Big Data, Data Analytics and other current developments will increasingly challenge the IT competence of controllers (see ▶ Sect. 5.1).

Traditionally, analytical skills and assertiveness are mentioned as interdisciplinary **key qualifications** for controllers. However, one should not underestimate skills that are more closely related to soft skills, such as listening, mediation skills and team skills. The development towards more soft factors is characterized by the observation that companies are managed more and better in consensus. This results in the fact that the old image of controllers as "bad guys" has become obsolete. The retreat of hierarchy requires more open and trusting communication. Especially for controllers it is therefore a key competence to get information and still be able to fulfill the role of rationality assurance of management, which necessarily includes the utterance of unpleasant truths. Otherwise, controlling quickly falls back into outdated role models such as the bean counter or number cruncher. This prejudice, which is still maintained in many companies, describes the controller as a numbers-obsessed and overly precise accountant who ignores the realities of business activity and instead strives for formal accuracy, the usefulness of which is more than doubtful (Weber and Schäffer 2020, p. 15).

Formally, most financial controllers require a university degree with a focus on business administration. This is supplemented by sound knowledge of the industry. In particular, if the image of the business partner is taken seriously, the latter is of fundamental importance. A controller can only be taken seriously if he understands how the actual business works. Only then can he give advice that meets the requirements of true rationality assurance. Otherwise, controlling quickly falls back into outdated role models such as the bean counter or number cruncher. This prejudice, which is still maintained in many companies, describes the controller as a numbers-obsessed and overly precise accountant who ignores the realities of business activity and instead strives for formal accuracy, the usefulness of which is more than doubtful (Weber and Schäffer 2020, p. 15).

1.5 Learning Control

To the point

In practice, controllers fulfill a variety of different tasks. Essentially, these can be divided into the areas of information management, planning, and project tasks. All of these tasks can be subsumed under the guiding principle of "securing rationality of management". Controlling is the department within a company that is responsible for ensuring that decisions are made rationally to the greatest extent possible. This task arises from the human limitation to act rationally (bounded rationality). In the best case, controlling can then assume the role of business partner, providing operational departments with expert knowledge as well as excellent business skills as consultant and partner for decision preparation.

Controlling departments can be classified as line (with decision-making competence) or administrative (with advisory competence only). Controlling is usually found on the first or second hierarchy level, with the first hierarchy level giving rise to the problem of the lack of independence in decision-making. In large companies, controlling can report centrally directly to the management or be placed decentralized in the individual business areas. Controlling is thereby located in the tension field between proximity to the business and independence, in order to also be able to express unpopular truths. Controllers usually have a completed university degree and good knowledge of accounting. In addition to assertiveness, the talent to gain trust is very important for success in the controlling function.

Let's check

Consider whether the following statements are true or false:

- Controllers are responsible for providing information to the management.
- Controllers decide on the content of corporate planning.
- Rationality means that with minimal resources a maximum result is achieved.
- Rationality means that with minimal resources a given goal is achieved.
- Information ensures that the uncertainty in decision-making is reduced.
- People are only limitedly rational because they do not know all relevant information, they do not know all possible actions and their consequences.
- Controllers act completely rational.
- If controlling is integrated within the line, it is especially independent from decisions.
- Even if controlling itself does not have decision-making competencies, it can exert a high amount of informal power through its role as decision-maker.
- Controlling should be represented directly in the board in order to be especially independent.
- In large companies, controlling can be organised centrally or decentralized.
- In the central organization form, the independent provision of information to the management is guaranteed.
- In the decentralized organization form, the proximity to the business activity is guaranteed, so that controlling can act as a good business partner.
- It is of particular importance for controllers to be able to enforce their decisions at any time.

Networking tasks

1. In a medium-sized engineering company with 100 employees, an independent controller position is to be filled for the first time. Consider how a job description (professional and non-professional skills) for this position should look.
2. Controllers should ensure the rationality of management. Consider which problems can arise in family-run businesses as opposed to companies whose shares are in public hands.

Read and deepen

- Weber and Schäffer(2020) Introduction to controlling. 16th edition, Schäffer-Poeschel, Stuttgart.
  Textbook that provides a basic introduction to all aspects of controlling. Weber and Schäffer are particularly responsible for the function attribution "Ensuring the rationality of management" for controlling. Otherwise, the basic questions of controlling are dealt with in detail here.
- Horváth et al. (2020) Controlling. 14th edition, Vahlen, Munich.
  Basic textbook on controlling. In addition to extensive historical introductions, the various concepts of controlling are presented in detail.

References

Behringer, S (2018) Konzerncontrolling. Springer

Becker W, Ulrich P, Botzkowski T (2016a) Controlling im Mittelstand. In: Becker W, Ulrich P (eds) Handbuch Controlling. Springer, Wiesbaden, pp 583–603

Britzelmaier B (2013) Controlling: Grundlagen, Praxis, Handlungsfelder. Pearson, München

Deimel K, Heupel T, Wiltiner K (2013) Controlling. Vahlen, München

Hopper TM (1980) Role conflicts of management accountants and their position within organization structures. Acc Organ Soc 5:401–411

Horváth P (2002) Controlling. In: Gaugler E, Köhler R (eds) Entwicklung der Betriebswirtschaftslehre. 100 Jahre Fachdisziplin. Schäffer-Poeschel, Stuttgart, pp 340–360

Horvath P, Gleich R, Seiter M (2020) Controlling, 14th edn. Vahlen, München

ICV (2013) Leitbild – Internationaler Controller Verein 2013. ► https://www.icv-controlling.com/de/verein/leitbild.html. Accessed 03 März 2017

Kosiol E (1967) Zur Problematik der Planung in der Unternehmung. Z Betriebswirtschaft 37:77–96

Lambert C, Sponem S (2012) Roles, authority and involvement of the management accounting function. A multiple case-study perspective. Eur Account Rev 21:565–589

Mintzberg H (2009) Management. Berrett-Koehler, San Francisco

Sanders K, Kianty A (2006) Organisationstheorien. VS, Wiesbaden

Simon H (1961) Administrative behavior, 2nd edn. Macmillan, New York

Stadermann HJ (1987) Ökonomische Vernunft. Wirtschaftswissenschaftliche Erfahrung und Wirtschaftspolitik in der Geschichte. Mohr, Tübingen

Ulrich P, Stier J (2020) Veränderung des Rollenprofils von Controllern in Folge der Digitalisierung. Control Mag 45:10–15

Weber J, Schäffer U (1999) Sicherstellung von Rationalität der Führung als Aufgabe des Controlling? DBW 59:731–747

Weber J, Schäffer U (2020) Einführung in das Controlling, 16th edn. Schäffer-Poeschel, Stuttgart

The Information Function of Controlling

Contents

S. Behringer, *Financial Controlling*,
https://doi.org/10.1007/978-3-658-40527-4_2

Learning Agenda

The information function of controlling is central to the assurance of rationality in leadership, as it is also the basis of the steering and control function. Controlling usually uses data from accounting, which is divided into external and internal. Controlling itself is often the carrier of internal accounting, but also has many relationships with external accounting, both as a user and as an information provider.

The basics of cost and performance accounting (internal accounting) are briefly explained, application areas are presented. The steering function of controlling offers the cost management, whose goal is to influence costs.

The main task of controlling in the information function is to prepare the information in such a way that it is decision-useful for the decision-makers in the company. For this purpose, controlling usually uses key figures or, if several key figures are combined, key figure systems, which are presented using selected examples.

The information function of controlling

Internal and external accounting as the basis of controlling	What tasks does internal and external accounting have? How do the two types of accounting differ?	▶ Sect. 2.1
Basics of cost and performance accounting	How is cost and performance accounting structured in the variant of full cost and partial cost accounting? What are the advantages and disadvantages of the two systems? Which business questions can be answered with both systems?	▶ Sect. 2.2
Cost management	What instruments can be used to control costs? What are the advantages of process cost accounting and target costing? For which problem areas are the two instruments suitable?	▶ Sect. 2.3
External accounting and controlling	What role does external accounting play for controlling? What information does controlling provide for external accounting?	▶ Sect. 2.4

2

Preparation of information on indicators and indicator systems	What is a key performance indicator? What functions do they take over? What are the success, financial and liquidity indicators and how are they calculated? How does the DuPont indicator system work? What is the Balanced Scorecard and what is to be considered when introducing it?	▶ Sect. 2.5

2.1 Internal and External Accounting as the Basis of Controlling

Accounting is a "systematic determination, preparation, presentation, analysis and evaluation of numbers on the individual business and its relationships with other economic subjects" (Weber and Rogler 2004, p. 2). Accounting is therefore a central part of the company's information system.

Accounting is divided into **financial accounting,** which is to be set up on the basis of legal (tax and commercial) obligations and also addresses external addressees, and **management accounting,** which is prepared for internal purposes and is addressed to a large extent to internal addressees. Financial accounting is the basis of external accounting, which culminates in the annual financial statements. Companies are obliged by national law to prepare financial statements. The legal basis for external accounting in Germany is the Commercial Code (HGB) and, in particular, the third book on commercial books. In Switzerland, the Art. 957 ff. of the Swiss Code of Obligations are decisive. In addition, the international accounting standards IFRS (International Financial Reporting Standards) are relevant for all companies in Germany whose securities are listed on a stock exchange or are in the process of being admitted to a stock exchange. These companies have to prepare their consolidated financial statements according to the international accounting standards.

Management accounting is the basis of internal accounting. It is also referred to as cost and performance accounting.

> In a nutshell: The internal accounting creates decision-making basis for the management of the company. The external accounting has outside the company's addressees and is intended to inform them about the company's situation. The external accounting is therefore based on statutory and other external rules.

The separation between external and internal accounting is based essentially on different relationships between the maker of the bill and the addressee (Ewert and Wagenhofer 2014, p. 4). In external accounting, the company is the maker of the worksheets. The addressees are different groups of people who regularly have significantly less information than the makers. In order to protect the less informed side, the legislature has enacted rules on how the external accounting is to be designed. In addition, the external accounting is the basis for the determination of the tax burden. Due to the different purposes of accounting, it can come to conflicts of interest, which makes it difficult, if not impossible, to use the external accounting for the purposes of controlling. This is different in internal accounting. The maker and the addressee are identical. There are no legal requirements, so that the management is free in the design of the worksheets. There may be conflicts of interest here too, but they are located within the company organization, for example in the conflict between different company departments.

The task of internal accounting is to support decisions within the company. Good decisions require good preparation and as broad and useful an information base as possible. In this respect, the internal accounting creates decision aids. With the help of calculation models, hopefully the most targeted decisions are made. Decisions are choice actions, i.e. there are at least two alternatives from which the decision-maker can choose. With the help of internal accounting, an aid should be created which of the actions available for the company is the best.

Costs and benefits are to be distinguished from **expenses and revenues**. The first mentioned term pair comes from internal and the second from external accounting. Both magnitudes arise basically from the same source, namely the accounting. The distinction is shown in ◘ Fig. 2.1.

Basic costs and operating expense are identical. If the expenses are greater than the costs, one speaks of neutral expenses. These expenses are taken into account in external accounting, but not set in cost and performance accounting. Neutral expenses can (cf. Schweitzer et al. 2016, pp. 41 f.) be unrelated to the main objective of the company, such as expenses for company sports or donations. Period-unrelated expenses, such as arrears for utility costs, belong in already closed accounting periods and would therefore distort the picture in the cost accounting. Extraordinary expenses have no relation to normal business activity, such as the flooding of a production plant. In addition, there is valuation-related neutral expenditure. This arises, for example, from legally binding different rules for external accounting. In Germany, for example, depreciation in external account-

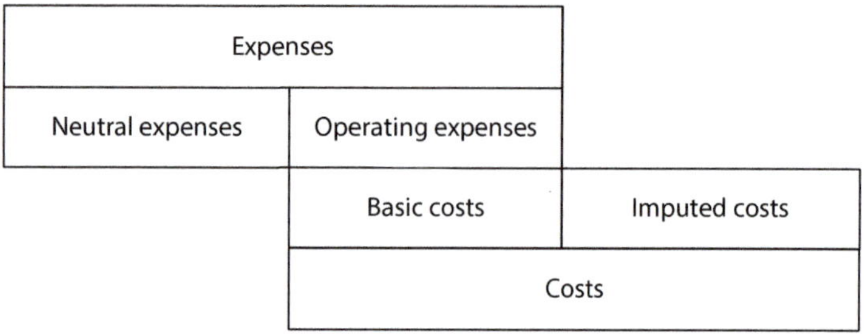

Fig. 2.1 Delineation of effort and cost. (Own representation based on Schweitzer et al. 2016, p. 41)

ing must be calculated from the historical acquisition costs. In internal accounting, however, it may make sense to take price increases into account in depreciation and to use the replacement costs as a starting point for the determination of depreciation.

If additional costs are included in internal accounting, this is referred to as imputed costs. Here one distinguishes between additional costs, which only exist in cost accounting in principle, and other costs, which exist in both external and internal accounting, but which differ in their amount. Additional costs include, for example, the calculative entrepreneur's wage (for employees of sole proprietorships or their family members), calculative rents (for buildings owned by the company itself) and calculative interest on the equity made available to the company by the owners. The basic idea of all additional costs is the idea of **opportunity costs**. If the entrepreneur did not work in his own company, he could receive a salary as an employee. The premises could be rented out to others, the equity could be invested elsewhere with interest income. In addition to costs that have no counterpart in external accounting, there are costs that are recorded there at a different amount. These are other costs. They are the counterpart to the valuation-related neutral expenses. They arise from standards that are prescribed for external accounting, but which are not considered to be appropriate for internal accounting.

There are a large number of connections and repercussions between internal and external accounting. In particular, the international accounting standards IFRS promote the harmonization of both worlds of accounting. The addressees of external accounting should receive an insight into the company "through the management eyes". This approach is referred to as the **management approach**. Companies should either adopt information directly from internal accounting or derive it from there. The idea of this approach is to install a reporting system that provides all addressees with tailor-made information regardless of the accounting standards. Information is then tailor-made if it is decision-supportive. Management wants to make decisions that contribute to the company's goals. However, this specification can indeed lead to goal conflicts that were not previously part of internal accounting, as ultimately all information is intended for publication at some point. In this way, the standards actually set the direction of unification: external accounting should approximate internal accounting and adopt its principles. In practice, however, the direction of unification is often the opposite. The provisions of external accounting are also used in internal accounting (Trapp 2012, pp. 254 ff.). The reason for this is that results can be planned and anticipated for publication.

2.2 Basics of Cost and Performance Accounting

2.2.1 Full Cost Accounting

Cost and performance accounting in the form of full cost accounting is divided into the following three sub-areas:

- **Cost type accounting:** It answers the question of which cost types have arisen, for example whether the costs were personnel or material costs.
- **Cost center accounting:** It breaks down the costs according to the place of their origin. A cost center is an organizational unit to which costs can be assigned. Often, the cost center breakdown of a company corresponds to the organizational structure as it is set out in the organizational chart. After the introduction of a cost center accounting, the question can be answered as to how many personnel costs have arisen in the personnel department. In cost center accounting, a distinction is made between main and auxiliary cost centers. Main cost centers are directly charged to the cost units (products or time units), while auxiliary cost centers are first allocated to main cost centers and thus only indirectly charged to cost units. Main cost centers are therefore departments that are directly attributable to a cost unit, such as product-specific sales. Auxiliary cost centers, on the other hand, are active for several cost units, such as the personnel department in a multi-product company.
- **Cost unit accounting:** In this part of the cost and performance accounting, the costs are assigned to calculation objects. Calculation objects can

be products on the one hand. This answers the question of which costs have arisen for the production of product XY. On the other hand, time units can be calculation objects. Then the question is answered of which costs have arisen in a time unit, e.g. an hour. The main problem with cost unit accounting is the attribution of costs to the cost carrier. With **indirect costs,** which cannot be directly assigned to a cost carrier, this is problematic and the subject of many discussions in companies, where controllers have to explain and defend their allocation keys. For example, the costs of the warehouse in a multi-product company cannot be clearly attributed to a single product as a cost carrier. Allocation principles (cf. Dierkes and Kloock 2002) are required. One possible principle that could be applied here is the **requirement principle**. According to this, the costs are charged as the cost unit has claimed the outgoing cost center. For the warehouse, this could be the space used, for example. The simpler **average cost principle** charges the respective costs with the same cost rates to the cost units. This promotes higher-value products, as they are burdened with indirect costs to the same extent as higher-value products. The viability principle, on the other hand, is based on the principle that those cost units should bear the most indirect costs that generate the highest revenues. None of these principles is right or wrong. Only the causation principle would be correct, but by definition it is not applicable to indirect costs—if the causation were to lie with the cost unit, these would be **specific costs** that can be directly attributed to a cost unit (e.g. the materials used). The **incurrence principle** is somewhat less strict. This states that the cost carrier should bear the costs that would not have arisen without him. But even this is hardly or not at all applicable to indirect costs. Since there is no right or wrong with the allocation principles, it should always be noted which behavioral effects arise from the choice of a principle. Sometimes high-quality products (average cost principle) are preferred, sometimes successful (average cost principle) and sometimes less successful (viability principle).

Cost and performance accounting is used in particular to determine prices and to calculate business success, for business planning or for special purposes such as determining basic values for investment calculations or for determining insurance values. There are relationships to the controlling functions in particular in the information function and the control function.

Cost and performance accounting uses various cost categories. **Actual costs** are the costs actually incurred that are determined for the past. Actual costs are important for the past-oriented determination of the success of a cost unit. However, they are less relevant for entrepreneurial decisions, since their consequences only arise in the future. In addition, there is no measure of whether the success was high or low. This can be changed by introducing **standard costs**. Standard costs are based on a normal level of employment and normal consumption of input factors. In practice, they are often determined by the average costs of the past, which are smoothed out by extraordinary events. With planned costs**,** the purely mathematical consideration, as it is carried out with standard costs, is supplemented by systematic considerations. For example, the costs of an operation are extrapolated on the basis of the costs of the previous period and supplemented by expected developments. This includes new hires, retirements, salary increases, and price developments. The Plankosten thus obtained can then actually be used as a measure for the actual costs. Typically, planned costs also serve as guidelines for the responsible persons of the cost centers.

2.2.2 Marginal Cost Accounting

Full cost accounting does not always lead to traceable results. This can be explained using an example: Let's imagine a cinema with 200 seats. The full cost of a performance is 1000 €. If the cinema sells the seats for 5 €, these self-costs would just be covered. But only 100 spectators come to the performance, the self-costs per seat increase to 10 €. If one were to base the price on this calculation and increase it by a profit margin, for example to 12 €, one might price oneself out of the market, as the price is no longer competitive with prices from other cinemas. If only one spectator comes, the self-costs per spectator are 1000 €. This result is obviously not suitable for use as a basis for price decisions.

Full cost accounting records all costs, the **fixed and the variable costs**. Fixed costs are those that are independent of actual employment. For the cinema performance, these are the hall rental, the license costs for the film, the staff etc. All of these costs arise independently of the number of spectators. Even if all costs—regardless of whether they are fixed or variable—have to be covered in the long run, there can be wrong decisions due to full cost accounting in the short term. The problems usually arise because the overhead costs are allocated to cost centers in full cost accounting. This can falsely give the impression that fixed overhead costs are variable costs.

In contrast, the marginal cost accounting only works with the variable costs. First, it must be decided which costs are variable and which are fixed costs **(cost allocation)**. There are various methods for this:

- The bookkeeping method uses observation of the cost behavior to determine whether it is fixed or variable costs. In addition, the character of the costs changes depending on the period under consideration. In the long term, all costs are variable. Personnel costs are variable if the periods under consideration are longer than the notice periods. The same applies to rental contracts.
- However, often cost types consist of both fixed and variable components. These can be determined using the minimax method. This assumes a linear cost function with the following form:

$$K(x) = k_v \cdot x + K_{fix}$$

The fixed costs are independent of the employment level. The cost increase from one employment level to the next must therefore be attributable entirely to the variable costs, which are assumed to be proportional.

▶ Example: Application of the minimax method in a production company

A production company has the following employment levels and total costs for its production:

Total costs at different production quantities

Month	Produced Quantity	Total Cost
April	400	50,000
May	600	70,000

To determine the variable components of production costs, the cost difference of 20,000 € is considered at an increased number of 200 units. This consideration results in variable costs of 100 € per unit. For the 400 units produced in April, the total variable costs are therefore 40,000 € and the fixed costs are 10,000 €. In May, the total variable costs are 60,000 € and the fixed costs are of course also 10,000 €. This can be expressed by the following cost function:

$$K(x) = 100 \cdot x + 10{,}000$$ ◀

However, costs often do not behave linearly. They can develop in a regressive (i.e. disproportionately falling with increasing production volume) or progressive (i.e. disproportionately rising with increasing production volume) manner. However, most of the time, the structure of the cost curve changes several times over the production volumes. In order to determine the split between fixed and variable costs, two data points are no longer sufficient. A cost function must be determined from as many data points as possible using regression analysis (cf. Britzelmaier 2013, pp. 112 ff.).

With the identification of fixed and variable costs, the conditions are created to design decision-making bases in such a way that the right measures can also be taken in the short term. The income statement in the system of partial cost accounting basically works in two steps:

1. Step:	Sales revenue—variable costs = contribution margin
2. Step:	Contribution margin—fixed costs = profit or loss

It can make sense to accept orders that only generate a contribution margin, but are overall loss-making. The reason for this is that a positive contribution margin contributes to the coverage of fixed costs and thus overall reduces the loss of a company or increases the profit. In the original example, the cinema operator has only fixed costs. Regardless of whether a visitor is sitting in the cinema or 200, his total costs are the same. The contribution margin of each visitor is therefore at the full ticket price. It is obvious that it would be wrong to reject the first visitor because in this case the loss through the screening is still very high (assumption: the ticket price is 8 €): With the first visitor, sales are 8 €, variable costs are 0. Consequently, the contribution margin is 8 €. However, the fixed costs are 1000 €, so that after the first visitor the total loss is 992 €. If the first visitor were rejected, the loss would still be 1000 €. On the other hand, an order must not be accepted or production must be stopped if negative contribution margins are generated. This would lead to an increase in the loss or a reduction in the profit.

Most companies have more than one cost unit and are hierarchically structured. Then the global treatment of all fixed costs, as was done in the above **single-stage contribution margin calculation,** is too short. As a result of this finding, the multi-stage contribution margin calculation was developed. Here, too, the variable costs are assigned to a cost unit. However, the variable costs are considered differently, depending on which level they were incurred. This can then lead to better decision-making when, for example, the decision is made to close a production area.

▶ Example: Multi-stage contribution margin calculation at Kitty Fitness GmbH

The company Kitty Fitness GmbH offers sports equipment. Under corporate management there are two areas. Area I deals with rowing machines. Area II deals with treadmills. The treadmill area is divided into two departments: Professional treadmills for fitness studios and treadmills for use in private households. In the department for treadmills in private households, the product "Couch Potato" is produced. The multi-stage contribution margin calculation for the treadmill "Couch Potato" has the following form:

1. Stage:	Sales revenues for the treadmill Couch Potato—variable costs of the product = Contribution margin I
2. Stage:	Contribution margin I—fixed costs for the product Couch Potato = Contribution margin II
3. Stage:	Contribution margin II—fixed costs of the department for treadmills in private households = Contribution margin III
4. Stage:	Contribution margin III—fixed costs of the area treadmills = Contribution margin IV
5. Stage:	Contribution margin IV—fixed costs of corporate management = Contribution margin V

From the second level, the results of the individual areas are summarized at each level. The number of levels in the multi-stage contribution margin calculation is not predetermined. It results from the organizational structure of the company. On each level, the decision maker receives information on how much is available to cover the still uncharged fixed costs or will lead to profit.

The Kitty Fitness GmbH can draw valuable conclusions from the multi-stage contribution margin calculation. If the individual products of the running machine department in private households have high contribution margins II, but the entire department only has a low contribution margin III, it must be clarified whether the fixed costs can be reduced at department level. If this is also not possible in the long term, the department should be considered for outsourcing. ◀

2.3 Cost Management

Cost accounting is concerned with capturing all costs and allocating them to cost units in a cause-and-effect manner. Cost management goes one step further. It seeks measures to control costs. Cost accounting is a prerequisite for good cost management, as decision-makers in companies need to know where costs have been incurred in order to shape them. In this respect, in addition to the information function, the steering function of controlling is also addressed in cost management.

2.3.1 Process Cost Accounting

In the 1980s, the increasing share of services in value creation in companies led to criticism of traditional cost accounting, which had been developed for industrial production companies (Brühl 2016, pp. 133 ff.). As indirect service areas such as quality management, logistics, purchasing etc. became increasingly important, the overhead costs and in particular the personnel costs became relatively more important in the total cost block. In order to still maintain meaningful figures, in particular the American practice developed process cost accounting, the Activity Based Costing. The purpose of cost accounting remains the same: decision-making basis for entrepreneurial decisions should be won. However, the cost allocation should be improved by a more traceable and ultimately more accurate classification.

In traditional cost accounting, cost centers are used to allocate overhead costs to cost centers and main cost centers to cost units—i.e. products. In process cost accounting, processes take the place of cost centers. This way, the path from undifferentiated allocation keys to cost allocation according to actual use is taken.

> In a nutshell: Activity-based costing supports a more cause-related allocation of overhead costs to individual cost carriers than traditional costing.

A significant further development of activity-based costing is that processes are also considered that extend across cost centers (Horvath et al. 1993, p. 617). Otherwise, activity-based costing is not a new development. It follows the traditional full costing in its structure with its division into cost type, cost center and cost carrier accounting.

Processes denote all activities in the company that are to produce a result. Typical processes are product development, procurement, production, quality assurance and sales. In the end, every service rendered in the company is created through processes. For the course of a process, an input is needed that is processed in the process itself and then leads to an output, the service. The processes are divided into:

1. **Main processes** that are rendered across multiple cost centers. They consist of
2. **Sub-processes** that are each carried out in a cost center.

A prerequisite for the meaningful formation of processes is that the services rendered are uniform and often repeated. If the processes are similar, the costs can be aggregated.

In ▪ Fig. 2.2 is an operation with two cost centers, each offering two sub-processes, shown. Cross-cost center, two main processes are assembled from them. One of them is fed by both sub-processes, which cost center 1 provides, and in addition by sub-process 2/2, which is provided by cost center 2. The second main process corresponds to sub-process 2/1.

Processes are then differentiated according to whether they are **quantity-induced** (lmi) or **quantity-neutral** (lmn). With lmi processes, process costs depend on the number of executions. Most of them have only little decision-making room in terms of costs, as the required quantities are predetermined, for example by recipes. The costs of lmn processes are independent of the performance volume. They are also referred to as structural or overhead costs. In the procurement department, for example, the process "manage department" is quantity-neutral. Meanwhile, the process "select suppliers" is quantity-induced. By him, higher costs arise whenever more suppliers have to be selected.

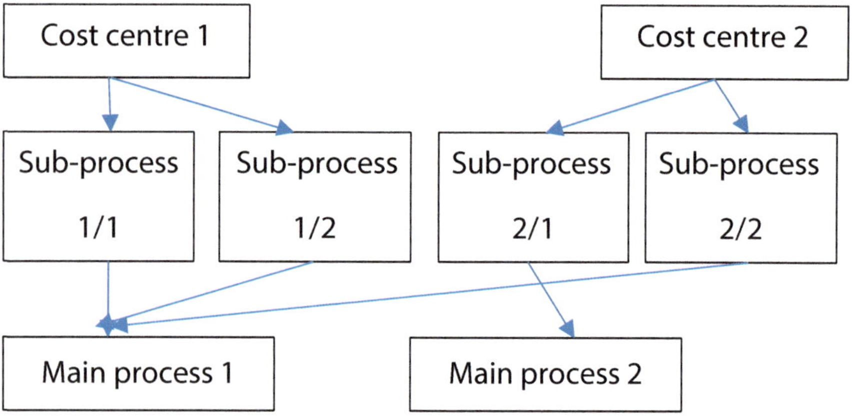

▪ **Fig. 2.2** Structuring of processes in process cost accounting

In order to characterize the costs and thus analyze them, the reference variables are determined for the processes, which influence the amount of the costs. They are referred to as **cost driver**. In the procurement department, cost drivers can be, for example, the number of deliveries, their volume or weight.

To the process cost rate one comes by dividing the costs of a process by the amount delivered. If the total costs of the process "procurement of consumables" are 1000 € and the number of deliveries has been determined as cost driver, then with 2000 deliveries a process cost rate of 0.50 € results. The formula for the calculation is:

$$\text{Process cost rate} = \frac{\text{Process costs}}{\text{Process quantity}}$$

This process cost rate is then used as the basis for the process to be charged to the cost carriers. In this way, the processes caused by the amount of performance can be distributed in a causative manner. This gives decision-makers the opportunity to control their cost burden. For example, if you bundle the procurement processes, the total costs of this process can be reduced. For the consumers of the sub-process "procurement of consumables", the burden is obviously clear through the attribution of costs, which should increase the incentive to take action. This is not so obvious with the performance-neutral processes. They are not essentially different in character than fixed costs. However, the process cost accounting provides the available data for calculations, for example in price decisions, more accurately.

An advantage of process cost accounting already occurs during implementation. By dealing with the processes in the company and their analysis, inefficiencies can be detected. The process cost rates determined can be used to think about rationalization up to outsourcing, for example if it becomes clear through the process cost rates that a service could be obtained much more economically on the external market. Of course, in addition to the purely cost considerations, other aspects must also be taken into account, such as quality, different services included, etc. This observation is also made in empirical studies on the success of the introduction of process cost accounting systems. A direct connection between company success and process cost accounting is not significantly detectable (this is also due to methodological problems, as it is difficult to isolate the effects of individual factors on company success). However, a connection was found between variables such as product quality, processing times or cost structure and the existence of a process cost accounting (Maiga and Jacobs 2008).

2

▶ Example: Process Cost Accounting at Kitty Fitness GmbH

The company Kitty Fitness GmbH ships its sports equipment from a central warehouse. The following three processes are carried out in this warehouse:

1. Department lead
2. Make storage
3. Send packages

Processes 2 and 3 are capacity-induced, while process 1 is independent of the actual shipped and stored amount. When the processes were first recorded, the four employees of the department were asked to write down the time shares used for the respective processes. These used capacities—represented as man-years—are therefore used as a key for the allocation of costs to the processes. The following costs arise for the processes:

Process costs for the warehouse of Kitty Fitness GmbH

Process		Dimension size		Key	Process costs			Process cost rate
			Quantity	Man Years	lmi	lmn	Total	
1	Leading a division	–		1.0		90,000		
2	Make deposits	Number of deposits	500	1.0	60,000	30,000	90,000	180
3	Sending packages	Number of packages	8000	2.0	120,000	60,000	180,000	22.50
Sum				4.0	180,000			

The procedure for the calculation is to be explained using an example, process 3 "ship packages". First, the total cost induced by the amount of work is distributed to the process using the key man-years. Process 3 uses a capacity of 2.0 man-years. This results in:

$$K_{lmi} = 180{,}000 \cdot \frac{2.0}{3.0} = 120{,}000$$

The total capacity for the amount of work-related processes is 3.0. The department head is not to be included, as the process "manage department", to which his capacity is to be attributed, is not related to the amount of work. The cost-neutral costs will also be charged to process 3 in the second step using the key man-years:

$$K_{lmn} = 90{,}000 \cdot \frac{2.0}{3.0} = 60{,}000$$

In the third step, the process cost rate is determined. For this purpose, the total costs must first be calculated as the sum of the amount of work-related and cost-neutral costs. These amount to 180,000 €. The process cost rate results from dividing these total costs by the total number of packages shipped:

$$k_P = \frac{180{,}000}{8000} = 22.50$$

This results in a process cost rate of 22.50. For each package shipped, 22.50 € are therefore charged to the cost units. This allows the responsible persons for the cost units to plan now. Even the head of the warehouse can now plan his costs. A deterioration in costs is at his expense (unless the reported quantities do not materialize). He is also responsible for any improvement in costs. ◀

2.3.2 Target Costing

Target Costing is strictly speaking not a separate cost accounting system. It uses other cost accounting systems for calculation. Basically, the usual procedure of cost accounting is reversed in Target Costing. First, a **realizable market price** is determined on the market from which a planned profit is deducted. This way, the maximum possible costs **(allowable costs)** are determined. These are then compared with the company's actual current self-costs **(drifting costs)**. These drifting costs are compared with the allowable costs. In most cases, the drifting costs will be higher than the allowable costs. In order to reach the previously determined target price, the costs must therefore be reduced. The maximum amount of costs to be achieved is called **target costs**. In the next step, the target costs are broken down into individual product components. From these component-specific target costs, the need for measures to be taken in order to achieve the price realizable on the market results. The schema illustrates ◘ Fig. 2.3.

Target Costing is characterized by a consistent market orientation. The question of traditional cost accounting "What does a product cost?" is changed to "What may a product cost?". The starting point for all considerations is therefore the benefit that a customer attributes to the product

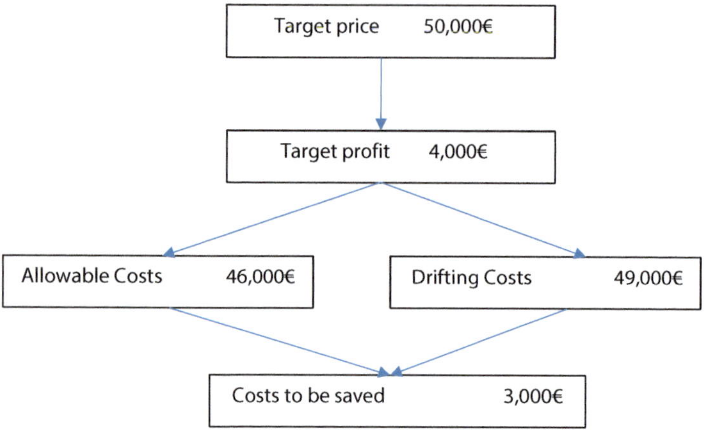

Fig. 2.3 Schematic procedure for Target Costing. (Own illustration based on Reichmann et al. 2017, p. 210)

and its properties and how much he is willing to pay for the individual components. Here the problem of this intuitively so convincing method begins. The determination of the necessary data is partly problematic.

> In a nutshell: Target Costing reverses the traditional view of cost accounting: The question is asked what a product may cost and not what it costs. This gives cost accounting a market orientation and supports the sales chances of new developments.

The market price can be obtained from market research data or from experience with similar products. However, the sales price of the product will change over its life cycle. If it is a completely new product, data is usually lacking, so that the method can be applied to product variants. It is also difficult to determine the target profit. The return on sales is usually used as a benchmark. This is defined as:

$$\text{Return on sales} = \frac{\text{Profit}}{\text{Sales}}$$

The costs are not yet known. The sales should be set so that a sufficient profit is made. Since the individual components are directly related to each other (profit is defined as sales minus costs), only heuristics can be used to obtain solutions (Ewert and Wagenhofer 2014, pp. 272 f.).

The costs that may arise along the value chain of the product can be determined in this way. The method is therefore suitable for cost management, i.e. it provides information about the need for cost reductions in certain areas, e.g. for the production of individual components that are incorporated into the product. But the insights from the user side are also important. It is significant for the manufacturer to see for which properties of a product the customer is willing to pay which amounts. The value contribution of individual components is determined with the help of conjoint analysis. This prevents over engineering of a product, i.e. very elaborate developments for which the customer is not willing to pay anything. If customers are not willing to pay the costs of a certain product component, the decision can be made to do without the production of this component.

The method of target costing originates from Japan and has established itself there, especially during the economic crisis of the 1990s. At that time, the yen gained value rapidly against the dollar, leading to greatly reduced profitability of the Japanese economy (Feil et al. 2004). In Japan, the instrument of target costing is linked to the concept of **kaizen,** continuous improvement. Target costing intervenes at the time of product introduction and supports the decision to develop a product or to do without development. Kaizen is constantly looking for opportunities for improvement and further opportunities to reduce production costs. The findings from target costing can be used to obtain starting points for the improvement process (cf. Horvath and Lamla 1996).

Empirical studies show that 60% of companies that have introduced a Target Costing process subsequently achieve target costs of at least 90%. However, there are significant differences in practice between German and Japanese companies. In Japanese companies, production-oriented departments such as design, product development, etc. are very involved, while in German companies financial controllers drive the processes (see Horvath and Tani 1997).

2.4 External Accounting and Controlling

The general norm of § 264 para. 2 sentence 1 of the German Commercial Code (HGB) describes the objective of the annual financial statements, the end product of external accounting:

2

> "The annual financial statements of the stock corporation are to give a true and fair view of the assets, financial position and earnings of the company in accordance with the principles of proper accounting."

The general norm of commercial law describes the purpose of accounting. The true and fair view is necessary in order to support stakeholders in their decision-making. For example, it is important for customers that the existence of the company is also secured in the medium term, in order to, for example, guarantee claims, updates or services in the future. Creditors and investors have an interest in financial stability, so that they know that their financial commitment is safe. In order to ensure this, it is necessary to prevent manipulation (Laux 1995, p. 419). In addition, the figures must also be comparable between companies, the same facts must be reflected in the same amount and in the same position in each annual financial statements. Only in this way can an investor find the right investment opportunity from different alternatives.

Not all specific business transactions can be regulated by law, there are always interpretative options. These use responsible corporate leaders to present their company better and to achieve their goals with stakeholders **(accounting policy)**. The question arises, therefore, whether external accounting is of importance for the purposes of controlling and thus for corporate management or whether, due to the statutory constraints of its design, it does not provide a decision-useful information base.

In terms of the annual financial statements, the management of a company occupies a special position. On the one hand, it is the source of information that goes into the annual financial statements. The management is responsible for deciding on the implementation of accounting policy measures, as well as for the accounting treatment of the facts and circumstances in view of the presentation of the company's assets, financial position and earnings. Furthermore, the management's expectations and plans enter the annual financial statements, for example when estimating provisions. These estimates are usually prepared by the controlling department. In addition, the management is also the author of the annual financial statements that is visible to the outside and represents this to the shareholders and other interested parties. In addition, the management is also the user of the information contained in the annual financial statements. For example, entrepreneurial decisions can be influenced by how they affect the annual financial statements (Eisenführ 1966, p. 33). The controlling department must take this relationship into account in its decision-making templates.

However, the role of the annual financial statements as an information tool of the management has changed a great deal in the view of business literature. Schmalenbach, the first professor of business administration at a German university, still considered the balance sheet to be the most important tool for business control (Schmalenbach 1962, pp. 49 ff.). However, the inevitable imprecision of the annual financial statements and its role for external stakeholders imply that the management will not base its decisions on the annual financial statements. The management has much deeper information than that which is published.

Nevertheless, the annual financial statements still play an important role in decision-making for management, even if no directly decision-useful information is found in the balance sheet or income statement. The annual financial statements are seen by external stakeholders as a benchmark for the company's performance and the quality of management. In this respect, the annual financial statements will also contain information for the management, namely the figures by which external observers measure efficiency. These data will, albeit with different weights, depending on the influence that outsiders can have on the position of the managers, be taken into account in the decision. The controlling department should take these factors into account in its decision-making templates.

In conclusion, it must be stated that the annual financial statements do not provide a sufficient information basis for the foundation of entrepreneurial decisions and can therefore by no means be the sole information basis for controlling. This is only possible with the help of internal accounting, which is based on a broader information basis and thus delivers results that are not intended for external stakeholders.

However, the basis for internal accounting results from financial accounting, since the basic costs correspond to the operating expenses. Therefore, the standards of external accounting are also contained in the figures of controlling. The controlling department must know this and take it into account in the preparation of information.

On the other hand, controlling, as the bearer of internal accounting, takes over various auxiliary tasks for external accounting. These are being expanded by the internationalization of accounting and the associated management approach. Traditionally, controlling, as the bearer of internal accounting, essentially fulfills the following three auxiliary functions for external accounting:

- Determination of the **production costs** for the valuation of self-made assets: For the valuation of such assets, rules are required, in particular with regard to which cost types may be included. Imputed costs (calculative interest, entrepreneur's salary, etc.) are not to be taken into account in any case, while individual costs (material individual costs, production wages, etc.) can be included without problems. The inclusion of overhead costs is difficult, as an allocation problem inevitably arises. § 255 para. 2 German Commercial Code (HGB) regulates that production-related overhead costs are to be included. A choice exists for a reasonable part of the general administrative costs and social benefits to employees if they have arisen during the production period. However, an inclusion prohibition exists for research and marketing costs. The determination of production costs requires support from cost and performance accounting. Different calculations can have a major impact on the success representation of the company: A stock valuation at full cost would result in a completely loss-free valuation, while costs that are not activated would each lead to an increase in the loss.

- **Valuation of self-made intangible assets of non-current assets:** With the German Accounting Modernization Act (BilMoG), which came into force in 2009, the German legislator created the choice in § 248 para. 2 HGB to activate self-made intangible assets (patents, software, etc.). In order to value the assets, it is necessary to determine the production costs for the balance sheet. These in turn originate from cost and performance accounting. According to IFRS (IAS 38), there is a duty to activate intangible assets of non-current assets, for which development expenses have to be set. Of the development expenses, research expenses have to be distinguished from research expenses. Research refers to the search for new knowledge, while development refers to the transfer of this knowledge into concrete products or the like. The activation of research expenses is therefore not allowed, as an immediate economic benefit cannot be proven. The consequence for controlling is that research and development have to be depicted separately, e.g. by two different cost centers.
- **Long-term production:** If an order extends beyond the accounting period, the question arises as to how this order is to be invoiced. In German commercial law, the general principle of the **Completed-Contract** method applies, i.e. a profit may only be realized when the order has been invoiced to the customer. This means that as long as the invoice has not yet been issued, the production costs must be activated. The long-term project must therefore become a cost bearer in the cost accounting in order to make the production costs always available. According to IFRS, the valuation is different: Here the **Percentage-of-Completion** method applies, according to which the success of a long-term

production order is to be reported on a pro rata basis. This also requires the pro rata recognition of revenues, which must then be offset against the corresponding production costs.

- In IFRS, controlling also has the task of providing assistance in determining **Fair Values** (Barth 2016, pp. 535 ff.). Fair Value is a predominant concept of IFRS, which is laid down centrally in IFRS 13.

Remember!

In IFRS 13, **Fair Value** is defined as "the price that would be achieved in an orderly transaction between market participants at the measurement date when selling an asset or when transferring a liability."

This is particularly true for the valuation of investments, but also for businesses, production facilities, etc. The concept is particularly important in the context of the acquisition of entire companies in consolidated financial statements. IFRS provides a hierarchy for valuation with fair value:

1. Preference should be given to actual market prices on active markets.
2. Observable factors should be taken into account, e.g. observable prices for similar assets.
3. Non-observable factors are used for valuation. The fair value is determined by a market-oriented valuation, e.g. by analytical valuations using the discounted cash flow method, but this must take into account all available information.

In particular, level 3 is mostly the responsibility of controlling. Through the management approach, the numbers must match those used elsewhere in controlling. In addition, the published segment reporting of external accounting must also be "through management eyes", i.e. the selected segmentation and the key figures used must correspond to those used in controlling.

2.5 Preparation of Information on Key Figures and Key Figure Systems

2.5.1 Basics of Key Figures and Key Figure Systems

Key figures are central to controlling. They represent quantitative data in condensed form in order to give an impression of reality, reduce complexity and make business-related matters transparent (Weber and Schäffer 2020, p. 171). The reduction in complexity is also associated with the fact that a key figure should reflect the essential aspects of a matter, but is not suitable for each individual case (Dellmann 2002, p. 941).

Since key figures are quantitative values, they must meet measurement requirements (Brühl 2016, p. 425). They must be valid and reliable. Validity means that a key figure actually measures what it is supposed to measure. For example, the key figure "absenteeism" can give an indication of the sick leave in the department. However, it is not necessarily suitable for something to say about the satisfaction of the employees in this department. Reliability means that the measurement of the key figure must be reliable. A key figure is then reliable if the measurement always leads to the same result under the same conditions.

Key figures can be differentiated into absolute and relative key figures. Absolute key figures, for example, provide information about the size of a company. Relative key figures are **ratio figures** that represent a further processing of the original data from external or internal accounting. Relative key figures have a higher informative value. For example, it cannot be seen from the turnover of a business year how the turnover has developed in comparison to the previous year. This can only be expressed by an index figure, such as turnover in relation to turnover of the previous year. Three types of relative key figures are distinguished (cf. Hauschildt 1971, pp. 340 ff.; Baetge 1998, pp. 26 ff.):

- **Proportional figures:** A sub-figure is set in relation to the corresponding total figure. For example, the equity ratio, which sets equity and total capital of a company in relation to each other, is a divisional figure.
- **Relational figures:** Here, relations are established between different types of figures. For example, the equity return on investment is a relational figure. It describes the ratio of annual profit and equity. Equity is the basic requirement for operating the company, so it is the cause of the success that has been achieved. Relational figures try to establish such cause-and-effect relationships between different figures.
- **Index figures:** Here, an absolute key figure is set in relation to the same figure at an earlier point in time. For example, the turnover in 2020 is set in relation to the turnover in 2019 and the change is calculated. It is important to note that the figures set in relation to each other must correspond temporally, materially and in terms of value, i.e. numerator and denominator must be equivalent. The periods of the two years must be of equal length. The underlying accounting standards must also be identical. In both cases, the turnover must be stated either net or gross.

In addition, when using index figures, care must be taken to ensure that an extraordinary year in which either particularly positive or negative events have occurred is not used as the base year.

In the literature, various functions are ascribed to indicators (cf. Weber and Schäffer 2020, pp. 173 ff.):

- **Stimulation function:** Indicators are used to stimulate initiatives to be taken and thus to eliminate irregularities and problems. This can go so far that the management of a company regularly takes a small selection of indicators, for example in the board meetings, and based on these indicators discusses questions of fundamental importance (cf. Simons 1995). This function of the indicators is very important for the role of the financial controller in the company. It gives him the opportunity to make recommendations for new initiatives that bring the indicators closer to the planned values.
- **Operationalization function:** Indicators are needed to make goals measurable. This is how the incentive systems for variable compensation in most companies are based on the achievement of indicators.
- **Prescriptive function:** In close connection to the operationalization function is the prescriptive function. Through indicators, critical goals are given as specifications for the operational units of the company down to individual employees. Indicators are therefore also used to motivate employees.
- **Steering function:** Here an indicator has the function of ensuring the control of systems in the company. This is how the various functional areas are to be coordinated and the interaction of different departments to be ensured. For example, indicators for inventory management are used in purchasing to decide whether new purchases should be made or not.
- **Control function:** In this function, indicators are used for target-actual comparisons. Based on this, deviation analyses can be carried out and corresponding initiatives for change can be started or sanctions imposed.

> In a nutshell: Indicators fulfill the stimulation, operationalization, specification and control functions in companies. They therefore play a central role in financial controlling.

In order to be able to approximate the real complexity of companies, in practice usually more than one key figure is needed. The selected key figures should be in a meaningful relationship to each other in order to not get contradictory or confusing statements. In this case, one speaks of a **key figure system**.

The unstructured determination of many key figures is problematic. The systematic collection of selected key figures avoids **information overload,** the overburdening of decision-makers with too much information, and makes the consistent interpretation of key figures easier. Systematics also includes a clear definition of key figures. Many companies understand key figures with different definitions under the same name. This not only makes it difficult to compare between companies. It also makes the interpretation of key figures by companies in controlling very difficult, because every controller and manager understands something different under the key figure and draws different conclusions from their development. Therefore, it is one of the extremely important tasks of controlling to specify clear definitions of the key figures used and to communicate them to the company.

In addition, too much focus on key figures can increase the short-term nature of decisions, as only the effect of a decision on the key figure is in focus. This is further reinforced by the fact that other non-monetary aspects may be neglected, which can have a negative impact on the quality of the decisions.

2.5.2 Success Indicators

Success indicators express the business success that a company has achieved in a period. The simplest key figure is the annual profit, the result of the profit and loss account before the use of results (distribution or accumulation).

Earnings before (EB) figures, which systematically omit (fully) non-management-influenced components, have become established in order to allow a better view of the management performance achieved: taxes (T as in Taxes), financial result (I as in Interest), depreciation on tangible fixed assets (D as in Depreciation) and depreciation on intangible fixed assets (A as in Amortisation). The omission of these result components is carried out in order to make companies comparable with different conditions (cf. Malik 2003). The most important of these figures are summarized in ◘ Table 2.1 below.

There are different tax systems in different countries. This effect is obscured by the omission of a company's taxes. International companies are comparable. Companies have different sources of financing, depending on whether they are, for example, a publicly traded company or a family-run

Table 2.1 Earnings before Kennzahlen

Kennzahl	Definition
EBT	Earnings before Tax = Net Income ± Extraordinary Expenses/Income + Taxes
EBIT	Earnings before Interest and Tax = Net Income ± Extraordinary Expenses/Income + Taxes ± Interest Expenses/-Income
EBITA	Earnings before Interest, Tax and Amortisation = Net Income ± Extraordinary Expenses/Income + Taxes ± Interest Expenses/-Income + Depreciation of Goodwill
EBITDA	Earnings before Interest, Tax and Depreciation = Net Income ± Extraordinary Expenses/Income + Taxes ± Interest Expenses/-Income + Depreciation of Goodwill + Depreciation of Fixed Assets

business. The financing situation and the associated interest burden are independent of the company's operational success. This imbalance is rectified by omitting the financial result. Depreciation is calculated according to different tax and commercial law rules, depending on the country of origin of a company. This is taken into account by omitting the depreciation component. Depreciation on intangible assets, such as goodwill, can be interpreted as special charges. This effect is also avoided by omitting it.

Earnings before interest and taxes have a great importance in the capital markets (see Hitz and Jenniges 2008, p. 237) and in the communication of companies with actual and potential investors. However, EBIT figures are not suitable for the operational management of companies. The purpose of omitting result components is to make different companies comparable. Controlling does not need this comparison within its own company—perhaps in a second step to **benchmarking,** that is, the comparison with other companies. Important information is lost by omitting it. A company with a very high EBITDA can still show a significantly negative, possibly even existential, annual deficit. Malik (see Malik 2003) ironically advocates, against the background of the widespread use of EBIT figures, that only one key figure is suitable for assessing a company, namely an EAE (Earnings After Everything).

Profitability ratios also belong to the performance indicators. They are relationship numbers that set the success of the company in relation to other variables. The **sales profitability** is mentioned:

$$\text{Return on sales} = \frac{\text{Profit}}{\text{Sales}} \cdot 100$$

The sales profitability (Return on Sales) shows how much profit remains from one euro in sales. The often used key figure EBIT is taken into account again in the numerator of the **EBIT margin** (see Dechene 2016, p. 475):

$$\text{EBIT margin} = \frac{\text{EBIT}}{\text{Sales}} \cdot 100$$

The EBIT margin shows how much of the sales remains as EBIT. This makes it possible to take into account the advantages of EBIT in the comparability of companies when analyzing profitability.

In practice, the **Return on Capital Employed (RoCE)** has established itself, which is used in particular by investment banks. The result is used in the numerator before interest. This ensures that the external capital providers are treated equally to the equity providers. Their compensation is not part of the annual surplus, as they only receive the distribution from this. On the other hand, the denominator is reduced by those liabilities that do not claim interest. These are in particular the liabilities from deliveries and services and the other liabilities. A supplier wants to receive the price owed at the payment date and does not claim any further interest. Formally, this results in:

$$\text{RoCE} = \frac{\text{Earnings before interest}}{\text{Total capital} - \text{non-interest-bearing liabilities}}$$

With the RoCE, financial controlling can calculate how much was earned with each euro of capital that is entitled to compensation. This also makes it possible to determine how much is available for the actual compensation of the capital providers. This key figure is of particular importance to potential equity and external capital providers, as they can see how much is theoretically available for their interest and dividend claims.

The **return on equity** was already mentioned as an example of a relationship number. It is calculated according to the following formula:

$$r_{\text{EK}} = \frac{\text{Annual profit}}{\text{Equity}}$$

The equity return is of particular importance to the equity providers, as it indicates how the capital made available by them has been interest-bearing. This allows the equity provider to compare this form of investment with other forms such as savings accounts with a bank or engagement with another company. The equity return can also be calculated with the EBIT instead of the annual surplus in the numerator.

2.5.3 Financial Ratios

Financial ratios are intended to help analyze the financial situation of the company. The financial structure of a company indicates how well protected the company is from a financial point of view in the event of insolvency. The key figure is the equity ratio, which was already introduced as an example of a breakdown number in ▶ Sect. 2.5.1. In this case, equity is set in relation to total capital. Since any loss is offset against equity, the equity ratio provides information on how many losses a company can still absorb and is therefore a measure of the financial security of the company (cf. Littkemann and Michalik 2004, p. 162).

The **debt-equity ratio** or debt-equity ratio is the mirror image of the company's indebtedness in relation to total capital:

$$\text{Debt ratio} = \frac{\text{Debt capital}}{\text{Total capital}}$$

Due to their mirror image, equity and debt ratios lead to the same statements about the financial stability of the company. However, it must be noted that security and profit-seeking are partly competing entrepreneurial objectives. Therefore, the statement that a high equity ratio or a low debt ratio is always good would be wrong. Rather, the optimal capital structure must be determined on a case-by-case basis depending on risk considerations, industry-specific factors and necessary financing options. For example, the use of debt can then increase the overall success of the company if the interest costs of the debt are lower than the return generated by the use of the capital in the company (leverage effect).

The **static debt ratio** looks at the ratio of debt to equity:

$$\text{Static debt ratio} = \frac{\text{Debt}}{\text{Equity}}$$

The static debt ratio can be seen as an indicator of a possible over-indebtedness of the company. Since the static debt ratio is derived purely from the balance sheet and thus from a purely past-oriented calculation, future developments and already fixed payments are not taken into account. The dynamic debt ratio tries to eliminate this deficiency.

$$\text{Dynamic debt ratio} = \frac{\text{Effective debt}}{\text{Operating cash flow}}$$

The numerator variable Effective Debt is defined as the company's liabilities plus the provisions minus the quickly liquidated assets (such as liquid assets, current assets). Operating cash flow refers to those receipts (i.e. liquid assets) that arise from the company's business activities (i.e. the normal sales process).

The statement of the dynamic debt ratio is the period of time the company needs to repay its existing effective debt from the operating cash flow (therefore, the dynamic debt ratio is sometimes also referred to as the "debt repayment period", Schult 1997, p. 161). A small dynamic debt ratio therefore means that the company can quickly repay its debts on its own and is therefore relatively independent of its creditors. However, it must be noted that all statements are based on the assumption that the company will generate the same operating cash flow in the future as in the past period.

2.5.4 Liquidity Ratios

Liquidity has two different meanings (Matschke 1991, pp. 26 ff.): On the one hand, it refers to the property of assets to be converted into cash (usually by selling). This is referred to as structural liquidity. On the other hand, however, dispositive liquidity refers to the ability of an economic subject, such as a company or a private individual, to meet its payment obligations punctually. The preservation of liquidity is of particular importance for companies, as illiquidity leads to insolvency (§ 17 InsO). The application can also be made by creditors. If insolvency is imminent, the company itself can file for insolvency due to impending insolvency.

> In a nutshell: Liquidity is the "conditio sine qua non" (necessary condition) of entrepreneurial action.

The liquidity of a company can be described with three **liquidity ratios**, which are differentiated according to the period under consideration. The period is determined on the one hand by how quickly the assets under consideration can be converted into liquidity (that is, how close they are to money) and thus used to settle liabilities. On the other hand, the maturity of the company's liabilities is considered. Both variables are set in relation to each other and give an indication of the company's liquidity situation. The short-term situation is described by liquidity 1st degree, which is also referred to as the cash ratio or bar liquidity:

$$\text{Liquidity 1st degree} = \frac{\text{Cash and cash equivalents}}{\text{Current liabilities}}$$

In this narrow sense, it is assumed that the company is only able to cover its short-term liabilities with the cash available at the moment. This is unrealistic, as almost every company is able to quickly increase its liquidity by selling assets that have a high proximity to money. In addition, requirements often lead to deposits that can then be used to settle own liabilities. This takes into account liquidity 2nd degree, which is also referred to as the quick ratio or acid test ratio:

$$\text{Liquidity 2nd degree} = \frac{(\text{cash and cash equivalents} + \text{current receivables} + \text{securities})}{\text{Current liabilities}}$$

Listed securities are usually easy to sell. At least part of the short-term receivables will lead to deposits. If liquidity 2nd degree is below 1, i.e. the liabilities are not completely covered by liquid funds and assets that can be quickly turned into cash, this may indicate short-term liquidity bottlenecks. The circle of assets to be considered is even wider with liquidity 3rd degree (current ratio). Here the whole current assets are used for comparison:

$$\text{Liquidity 3rd degree} = \frac{\text{Current assets}}{\text{Current liabilities}}$$

If the liquidity of 3rd degree is less than 1, the current assets do not cover the short-term liabilities. There is a danger that fixed assets, which are actually intended to serve the company in the long term, have to be sold to settle the short-term liabilities. US banks use the Two-to-One-Rule or Banker's rule when granting loans (Mensch 2002, p. 181), according to which the liquidity of 3rd degree must be 2.

The liquidity ratios give an important impression of the liquidity situation of a company. However, it is critical to note that the due dates of the numerator and denominator do not have to be exactly the same. In particular, important and high sums may be missing from the payment obligations, as these are obligations that are not due at the time of the balance sheet and therefore may not be included in the balance sheet. This is the case, for example, with salary payments or interest payments.

In addition to the liquidity analysis of companies, the key figure **Working Capital** originating from the Anglo-American area is particularly used. It is formed as the difference between short-term assets (current assets) and short-term liabilities (each with a maturity of up to one year). The background of this calculation is the timely financing: short-term assets should also be financed short-term. The key figure should normally be positive, i.e. the short-term assets should exceed the short-term liabilities. If this is the case, the short-term liabilities can be covered by selling the short-term assets (cf. Deimel et al. 2013, p. 194). However, this should not be misunderstood as an invitation to maximize working capital. Too much working capital leads to excessive capital commitment. Meanwhile, a whole sub-discipline of financial controlling, working capital management, is dealing with the complex task of optimizing working capital (cf. Meyer 2007 and others). It is immediately clear that, for example, too high inventory or too high receivables are not positive for the company. In particular, receivables and inventories should be optimized. The average receivables period is calculated for receivables (Days Sales Outstanding, DSO):

$$\text{DSO} = \frac{\text{Receivables from deliveries and services} \cdot 360}{\text{Sales}}$$

The DSO shows how long (in days) the company has to wait on average for its money from sales revenues. Starting points to improve this key figure are to improve dunning and collection.

Another important key figure for liquidity is the inventory range DIH (Days Inventory Held). It indicates how long the company's inventories will last to sell the products sold on average in the past:

$$\text{DIH} = \frac{\text{average inventories} \cdot 360}{\text{Cost of materials}}$$

The DIH should not only be minimized mathematically. However, the decisive condition is that the company retains its delivery capability. If an order cannot be carried out due to a lack of stocks, it can be assumed that the turnover is finally lost, since the potential customer will obtain the delivery elsewhere.

2.5.5 The DuPont Analysis

The DuPont Analysis was the first **performance management system** in history to be used in corporate practice. It was used in 1919 by the American chemical company E. I. du Pont de Nemours and Company. The background was the invention of the strategy of the multidivisional corporation.

General Motors is considered to be the first company to divide its various activities into divisions, that is, independent and relatively autonomous organizational units: cars with different brands, trucks and spare parts. This strategy is essentially due to the then chairman of General Motors Alfred Sloane. A second influential figure was the most important owner of General Motors in the 1920s, Pierre du Pont, who also owned the chemical company DuPont. Divisions were also formed in his chemical company with managers who were responsible for their division (cf. Micklethwait and Woolridge 2003, pp. 104 ff.). In order to assess the success of the divisions and to see which divisions should receive additional financial resources, it was necessary to have a system of assessment, which was created and used with the development and use of the DuPont Performance System. ◘ Figure 2.4 shows the DuPont Performance System graphically.

The starting point is the realization that maximizing an absolute value such as profit alone is not productive. Instead, a relative value, the **Return on Investment (RoI),** is chosen as the top metric. This size is decomposed into its mathematical elements in the performance measurement system, so that the factors influencing the company's business activity become visible. This makes it possible to identify weaknesses across divisions or companies by comparing performance indicators and to initiate appropriate countermeasures. By relating to a reference value, size-specific factors are no longer taken into account in the further assessment: companies of different sizes are comparable. The mathematical decomposition of the top metric into the individual elements helps to reveal the options for action to increase the success of the company.

The return on investment shows how much has been earned with the invested capital. The size RoI is divided into the multiplicatively linked sizes **sales profitability and turnover**. The sales profitability shows how much of a euro sales remains as a percentage of profit. The indicator therefore shows how the money has been earned. In the further divisions of the sales profitability metric, the individual factors that influence success are made transparent. The upper strand of the DuPont system is fed by the sizes of the profit and loss account. In contrast, the lower strand is mainly fed by balance sheet values. They represent the sources from which the income comes. The lower strand can therefore be interpreted as an expression of the goal "secure income sources" (cf. Baetge 1998, p. 522), since the balance sheet contains those assets with which the company generates the profit.

As the metric makes clear, the RoI can be increased in two ways. If you choose sales margin as the starting point, cost savings or sales increases can lead to an improved RoI while the other size remains constant. While these

2

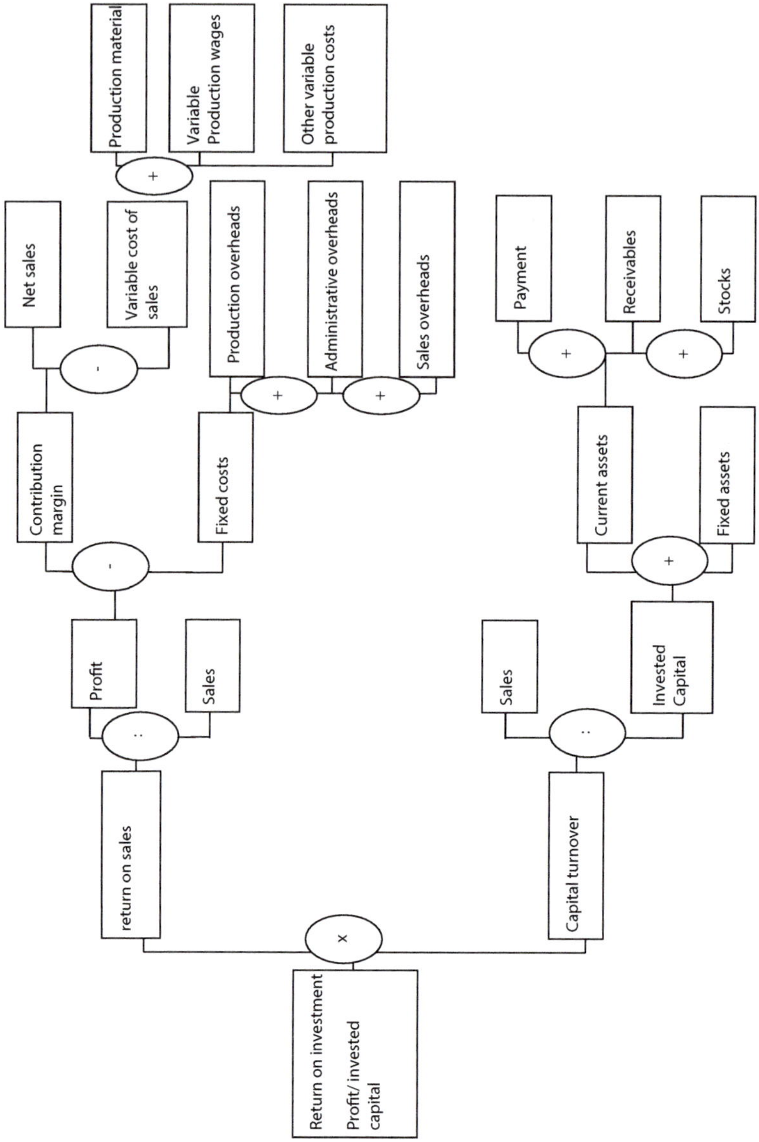

Fig. 2.4 The DuPont Analysis. (Source: Behringer 2018, p. 113)

measures are obvious, this is not necessarily the case with the second approach: a reduction in the capital employed leads to an increase in the turnover and thus to an increase in the RoI. This can support working capital management. For example, a reduction in inventory levels leads to a reduction in the capital employed and thus to an increase in the RoI.

The manager of a division is given a great deal of freedom of action with the DuPont performance measurement system. The predetermined return on investment is set for him by target agreement within the framework of management by objectives. It is also advantageous that the company's return on investment goal is not lost sight of and that the division of the return on investment makes it possible to identify causes of deviations (cf. Zünd 1973, pp. 127 f.). On the other hand, the strong mathematical connection between the performance indicators suggests the existence of a mechanical system. However, this mechanical view is not appropriate due to the strong and rapid changes to which companies are exposed.

It is critical to note that the DuPont performance measurement system is based solely on financial indicators. This means that areas that are outside the financial sphere of the company but can still be very important are not considered. In this respect, the DuPont performance measurement system must be described as unbalanced. Since the starting point is the external accounting system, this also includes measures to manipulate the balance sheet. The system can therefore become innovation-inhibiting because non-activated innovations are only considered as expenses and thus reduce the return on investment in the short term. Only in the following period do innovations lead to sales revenues, which in turn increase the return on investment.

Due to the commitment to the return on investment, the heads of divisions are autonomous in their decisions, as the corporate headquarters only refers to the return on investment after a period has expired. However, this autonomy can also have disadvantages for the entire company. Let's assume that a company consists of two divisions. One—production of strawberry jam—has a return on investment of 10% and the other—production of orange jam—a return of 20% and both divisional managers are each measured by the return on investment generated. The head of the production of orange marmalade would reject an order that has a return of 15%, even though this order would increase the overall success of the company. However, the return on investment for orange marmalade would decrease, which would prompt him to reject it.

2.5.6 The Balanced Scorecard

In contrast to the DuPont scheme, the balanced scorecard is a **balanced performance measurement system** that extends the financial perspective to other perspectives that are important for corporate management. The balanced scorecard is a tool of strategic controlling, as all performance indicators should have a reference to the company's strategy. In particular, the balanced scorecard should help to communicate the strategy. First, the company's strategy must be formulated, which is then operationalized by performance indicators. It is assumed that many executives do not know the strategy or only have a vague idea of the measures for its implementation. The performance indicators, which become elements of the balanced scorecard, should improve this communication process.

It was crucial in the development to realize that purely financial indicators were sufficient for the industrial era, but in the knowledge society with shorter product life cycles and international competition, other requirements for corporate governance are important. The inventors Kaplan and Norton have symbolically shaped the image of a pilot who also needs various information about altitude, speed, fuel consumption, distance to the target, weather conditions to safely bring the plane to the target. A pilot who would get his information from a single instrument would not be trusted and thankfully decline the flight (cf. Kaplan and Norton 1996, p. 1). Nor can a company manager be able to run a company with only one indicator. Rather, he must juggle different balls in his hand that he must observe with suitable indicators. Specifically, the Balanced Scorecard complements the financial perspective with a customer, an internal process and a learning and development perspective, all of which relate to the company's strategy (cf. Kaplan and Norton 1996, pp. 24 ff.):

- The **financial perspective** comprises purely monetary indicators. Typically, the period profit, the RoI or the sales margin are used. Even in the model of the Balanced Scorecard, the financial perspective retains a superior role. On the one hand, it clarifies which monetary contribution a strategy has made to the financial success of the company as a whole. On the other hand, the financial perspective also represents the final goal for the other perspectives. All indicators in the Balanced Scorecard must be linked to each other by **cause-effect relationships,** with ultimately all contributing to financial success. The financial perspective should answer the question of how the company should behave towards its owners in order to achieve financial success.

- The **customer perspective** looks at the company from the market. Here, for example, market share, customer satisfaction or customer loyalty indicators can be used. The goal is to find out how customers see the company. As an early warning system, problems in the market should be detected that would only be reflected in the financial figures after the risk had occurred (e.g. in lower sales because customers are not satisfied with the company). The indicator "number of customer complaints" can be seen in time that the customers begin to be dissatisfied. The customer perspective should answer the question of how the company should behave towards its customers in order to realize its vision.
- The **internal process perspective** deals with all internal processes that are necessary to achieve the financial and customer-related goals. Performance indicators such as the time required to bring new products to market (time to market), capacity utilization, scrap rates or productivity can be used. This makes it possible to detect early on that processes are running poorly, which will eventually lead to customer dissatisfaction. The focus of this strategy is the question of which business processes one has to be the best in order to satisfy the shareholders and customers.
- The **learning and development perspective** shows the potentials that need to be developed in order to achieve the goals in the first three perspectives. These include investments in employee training, investments in research and development or in information technology. Employee satisfaction, turnover or innovations made by the company can be measured. This is an early warning system for process deterioration. Poorly qualified employees will be able to deteriorate processes in the future. The question should be answered how the change and growth potentials should be promoted in order to realize the vision.

◘ Figure 2.5 shows the schema of the Balanced Scorecard.

In addition to financial indicators, business-specific indicators are usually also mentioned, which are also referred to as **performance drivers** (cf. Weber and Schäffer 2020, p. 194). Financial indicators, on the other hand, are result indicators that show the result achieved afterwards. Performance drivers provide early information on developments and enable the company to react early to changes. Sales are a result figure that says how many customers have bought, customer satisfaction is a performance driver that can give information about how sales will develop in the future.

In order to meet the oversupply of information that is common in everyday business life, the Balanced Scorecard requires a clear limitation of the

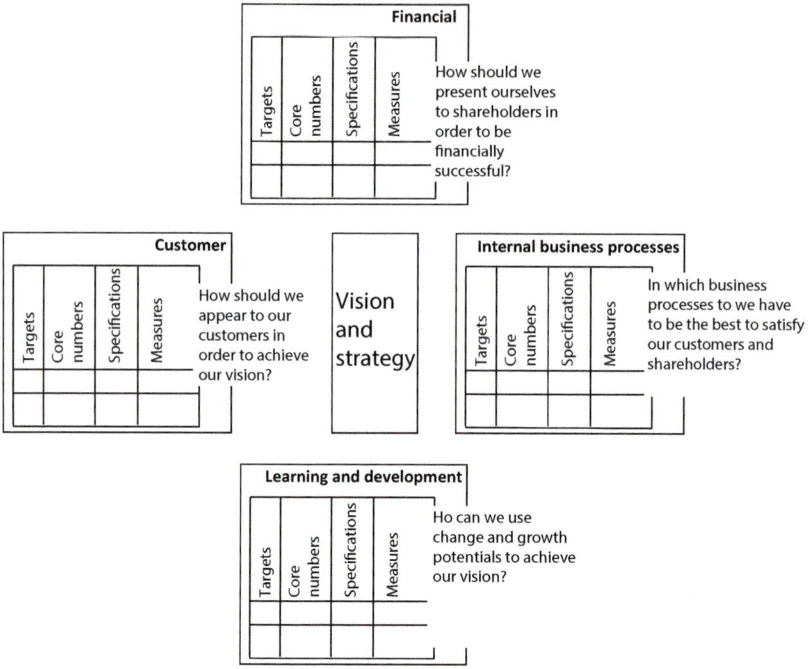

Fig. 2.5 The Balanced Scorecard. (Own representation based on Kaplan and Norton 1996, p. 9)

indicators used to approximately five per perspective. This ensures that what is important can be distinguished from what is unimportant. However, the restriction to four perspectives is not mandatory. Specific additional perspectives can be added (cf. Kaplan and Norton 1996, p. 34). For example, it is proposed to add a fifth perspective "sustainability" in order to take into account the increasing importance of sustainable economic activity in corporate policy (cf. Epstein and Wisner 2001).

Two criteria are generally used for the specific selection of indicators. Each indicator must have a strategic reference, i.e. it must have an impact on the success of the company. In addition, the indicators must be influenced by management. All indicators should be linked to each other by a cause-and-effect relationship. Unlike the DuPont analysis, this does not involve mathematical, but rather logical connections.

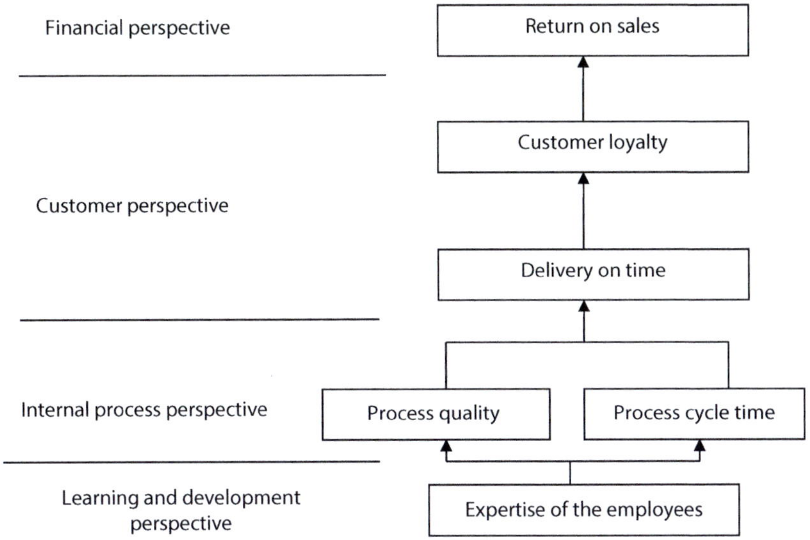

Fig. 2.6 Cause-effect chain in the Balanced Scorecard. (Own illustration based on Kaplan and Norton 1996, p. 31)

One possible cause-effect chain (Fig. 2.6) assumes that higher expertise of employees leads to higher process quality and thus to shorter process cycle times. This in turn results in the company being able to deliver on time, which leads to higher customer satisfaction. Customer satisfaction in turn leads to customers returning and placing further orders, which increases the financial success of the company, which can be measured, for example, by the sales margin. However, one must be careful that there is by no means an automatism here. So higher process quality can indeed lead to slower cycle times and thus to a tendentially less punctual delivery (cf. Wall 2001, pp. 69 ff.), since more thoroughness or more controls are built in.

In practice, it turns out to be difficult to identify cause-effect chains. One is dependent on experience, which can often be misleading. Correlations—the analysis of which Kaplan and Norton suggest for the identification of cause-effect relationships—must not be confused with causality (Brühl 2015, pp. 196 f.). Furthermore, the costs of individual measures can often be assigned. So it is easy to attribute the training costs of a department. However, it is difficult to divide the revenues accordingly. The question of how many revenues have been generated by the training measure of a sales representative cannot simply be answered. However, this would be necessary to derive causality for the Balanced Scorecard.

> In a nutshell: To introduce a balanced scorecard, the following six steps are required (see Gleich 2011, p. 80):
>
> 1. Formulate the company's vision.
> 2. Formulate strategy and strategic goals.
> 3. Select indicators that fit the formulated strategy (valid and reliable).
> 4. Find cause-and-effect chains that map the relationships between strategic goals and indicators.
> 5. Include indicators in the balanced scorecard.
> 6. Specify concrete manifestations for the strategic goals and the selected indicators.

The connection of operational and strategic elements is achieved through cause-effect chains. In practice, many indicators that are part of the scorecard are taken from the field of operational management. This is also sensible, as only in this way can the early warning function actually be assumed. The departure from the purely financial point of view also helps here: The financial success variables can only be actually influenced by the employees at a high level, but non-financial variables from the process, customer or learning and development perspective can indeed be influenced by employees of all hierarchy levels in the operational area. This also makes the contribution of these hierarchy levels to the company strategy clearer.

Kaplan and Norton do not understand the Balanced Scorecard solely as an instrument for result measurement. They rather understand it as an instrument for the implementation of strategies. An application is therefore only sensible if a strategy has been formulated. In a first step, goals have to be formulated that concretize the implementation of the strategy. The indicators to be selected in the second step, which are represented in the Balanced Scorecard, must be closely related to these goals and must be understood as a measure of goal achievement. In the Balanced Scorecard, the actual values of the indicators are then measured and compared with the target values. Finally, measures must be derived as to how the discrepancy between target and actual value can be reduced or eliminated **(Action Control)**. It is important here that the goal of a Balanced Scorecard should go beyond measurement and control, as traditional key figure systems provide for it. Communication, learning and information are to be achieved by the scorecard (Kaplan and Norton 1996, p. 56), for example by regularly communicating the indicators and their status to all employees.

In order to be able to fulfill the function of strategy implementation, the Balanced Scorecard should also be used in the assessment of variable compensation (cf. Kaplan and Norton 2001). In this way, the strategic goal can also be taken into account operatively in the middle management area. The Balanced Scorecard is a simple means by which these goals can be conveyed to the employees. However, this requires that objectively measurable indicators are used and no indicators whose measurement depends heavily on the goodwill of the assessing manager.

The introduction of a Balanced Scorecard is associated with a variety of changes in the incentive structures for all employees. For this reason, introduction projects are often associated with acceptance problems. In particular, if variable compensation is actually linked to the Balanced Scorecard. The order for an introduction can therefore only come from the top management of the company. The involvement of consultants can be useful in order to ensure an objective view from outside the company.

Even though the Balanced Scorecard has found a great deal of dissemination and followership throughout management literature, its practical application is significantly lower. An empirical study (cf. Speckbacher et al. 2003) has shown that of the 200 largest German stock corporations, only 24% use the Balanced Scorecard and only 7% apply it as an instrument of strategic management. A survey of 260 large companies yielded an application rate of 60% (Horvath and Partner 2011). In particular, the use of cause-and-effect relationships poses problems for companies. 42% of companies therefore do without the application of these chains (cf. Bach 2006).

2.6 Learning Control

Concise and to the point

The information function is central to financial controlling, as the other controlling functions are based on it. The main source of information is accounting, which is divided into external (in accordance with statutory requirements to third parties outside the company) and internal accounting, which is addressed to the management of the company. Internal accounting is also referred to as cost and performance accounting. In the traditional view, the incurred costs are allocated to the cost units (products, time units) in a cause-and-effect manner. In certain situations, full cost accounting proves to be unsuitable for the preparation of decision-making bases, which is why marginal cost accounting was developed, which only takes into account fixed costs in different stages (contribution margin accounting).

Modern forms of cost and performance accounting are not only concerned with the recording of incurred costs, but also want to contribute to the steering function of controlling. Process cost accounting strives to allocate common costs to cost bearers in a cause-and-effect manner and to identify potential for cost optimization at an early stage. Target costing starts from the maximum price that can be imposed on the market and determines the highest sustainable costs.

Information is processed into key figures and key figure systems. They help decision-makers to quickly and accurately identify which development the company is taking or has taken. This makes decision-making in the company easier. Often, the focus on a single key figure is not enough, as it does not completely reflect the situation. For this reason, key figure systems such as the DuPont analysis have been developed. The Balanced Scorecard is a key figure system that belongs to strategic controlling. Non-financial key figures are also used here, which are intended to help identify misdevelopments before they are reflected in the figures of accounting.

Let's check

Consider whether the following statements are true or false:

- Companies must maintain an internal accounting system to meet legal requirements.
- According to IFRS, internal and external accounting grow together through the management approach.
- Cost accounting distributes the incurred costs to products.
- In short-term price decisions and high fixed costs, marginal cost accounting leads to better results than full cost accounting.
- If the contribution margin I is negative in the multi-stage contribution margin accounting, the company should strive for higher sales volumes.
- In activity-based costing, overheads are charged more fairly to cost objects through process view.
- Target Costing reverses the traditional cost accounting view: The maximum bearable costs are calculated, not the incurred costs.
- The fair value according to IFRS must always be calculated analytically by controlling when there are no market prices (or comparable prices cannot be determined).
- Ratios express two different magnitudes in relation to each other.
- Often, performance measurement systems lead to better decision-making because individual performance measures are too simplified.
- The liquidity 1st degree should be 3 or more.

- When considering EBIT, companies of different nationalities can be better compared.
- RoI is the top metric in the DuPont analysis.
- Only financial metrics are used in the Balanced Scorecard.

Networking tasks

1. It has been shown how marginal cost accounting can support better decisions in the short term. Consider the disadvantages that can arise from the sole use of marginal cost accounting in a company on the market!
2. Identify possible meaningful metrics for the four perspectives of the Balanced Scorecard for an online fashion retail company!
3. Put together examples in which (in German GAAP) choice rights can distort the annual financial statements from external accounting as an information basis for operational decisions!

Read and deepen

- Schweitzer et al. (2016) Systeme der Kosten- und Erlösrechnung. 11th edition, Vahlen, Munich.
  The book explains cost and revenue accounting as the basis of controlling in detail and with all modern developments.
- Reichmann et al. (2017) Controlling mit Kennzahlen. 9th edition, Vahlen, Munich.
  This work describes the derivation and interpretation of key figures as a key function of controlling. Here you will find detailed explanations of the most important key figure concepts.
- Brösel, G (2017) Bilanzanalyse. Unternehmensbeurteilung auf der Basis von HGB- und IFRS-Abschlüssen 16th edition, Erich Schmidt Verlag, Berlin.
  This book emphasizes the anchoring of key figures in external accounting. It is therefore suitable for deepening students who have already dealt with the questions of external accounting.

References

Bach N (2006) Analyse der empirischen Balanced Scorecard Forschung im deutschsprachigen Raum. Control Manag 50:298–304

Baetge J (1998) Bilanzanalyse. IDW-Verlag, Düsseldorf

Barth T (2016) Planung im Zusammenhang mit der Bilanzierung und Bewertung nach IFRS. In: Becker W, Ulrich P (eds) Handbuch Controlling. Springer, Wiesbaden, pp 529–549

Behringer S (2018) Konzerncontrolling, 3rd edn. Springer, Wiesbaden
Britzelmaier B (2013) Controlling: Grundlagen, Praxis, Handlungsfelder. Pearson, München
Brühl R (2015) Wie Wissenschaft Wissen schafft. UVK, Konstanz
Brühl R (2016) Controlling. Grundlagen einer erfolgsorientierten Unternehmenssteuerung, 4th edn. Vahlen, München
Dechene C (2016) Bilanzkennzahlen und Bilanzanalyse. WISU 44:469–476
Deimel K, Heupel T, Wiltiner K (2013) Controlling. Vahlen, München
Dellmann K (2002) Kennzahlen und Kennzahlensysteme. In: Küpper HU, Wagenhofer A (eds) Handwörterbuch Unternehmensrechnung und Controlling, 4th edn. Schäffer-Poeschel, Stuttgart, pp 940–950
Dierkes S, Kloock J (2002) Kostenzurechnung. In: Küpper HU, Wagenhofer A (eds) Handwörterbuch Unternehmensrechnung und Controlling, 4th edn. Schäffer-Poeschel, Stuttgart, pp 1177–1186
Eisenführ F (1966) Anforderungen an den Informationsgehalt kaufmännischer Jahresabschlußrechnungen. Diss., Kiel
Epstein MJ, Wisner PS (2001) Using a balanced scorecard to implement sustainability. Environ Qual Manag:1–10. ► https://doi.org/10.1002/tqem.1300
Ewert R, Wagenhofer A (2014) Interne Unternehmensrechnung, 8th edn. Springer, Berlin
Feil P, Yook K-H, Kim I-W (2004) Japanese target costing: a historical perspective. Int J Strateg Cost Manag 5:10–19
Gleich R (2011) Performance Measurement: Konzepte, Fallstudien und Grundschema für die Praxis, 2nd edn. Vahlen, München
Hauschildt J (1971) Entwicklungslinien der Bilanzanalyse. Z Betriebswirtsch Forsch 33:335–351
Hitz JM, Jenniges V (2008) Publizität von Pro-forma-Ergebnisgrößen am deutschen Kapitalmarkt. Z Intern Kapitalmarktorientierte Rechn 2008(4):236–245
Horváth & Partner (2011) Performance management im Einkauf 2011: den Wertbeitrag des Einkaufs aktiv steuern und optimieren. Horvath & Partner, Stuttgart
Horvath P, Lamla J (1996) Kaizen Costing. krp 40:225–240
Horvath P, Tani T (1997) Japanese-German comparison of target cost management. Working paper
Horvath P, Kieninger M, Mayer R, Schminak C (1993) Prozeßkostenrechnung – oder wie die Praxis die Theorie überholt. DBW 53:609–628
Kaplan RS, Norton DP (1996) Translating strategy into action: the balanced scorecard. Harvard Business School Press, Boston
Kaplan RS, Norton DP (2001) Transforming the balanced scorecard from performance measurement to strategic management. Account Horiz 15:147–160
Laux H (1995) Erfolgssteuerung und Organisation. Springer, Heidelberg
Littkemann J, Michalik C (2004) Instrumente des operativen Beteiligungscontrollings. In: Littkemann J, Zündorf H (eds) Beteiligungscontrolling. Neue Wirtschafts-Briefe, Herne, pp 146–167
Maiga AS, Jacobs FA (2008) Extent of ABC use and its consequences. Contemp Account Res 14:533–566
Malik F (2003) Gefährliche Worte. Manag Mag 2003(12):98
Matschke MJ (1991) Finanzierung der Unternehmen. nwb, Herne
Mensch G (2002) Finanz-Controlling. In: Finanzplanung und -kontrolle. Oldenbourg, München

Meyer CA (2007) Working Capital und Unternehmenswert. Gabler, Wiesbaden

Micklethwait J, Woolridge A (2003) The company. A short history of a revolutionary idea. Modern Library, London

Reichmann T, Kißler M, Baumöl U (2017) Controlling mit Kennzahlen, 9th edn. Vahlen, München

Schmalenbach E (1962) Dynamische Bilanz, 13th edn. Westdeutscher Verlag, Köln

Schult E (1997) Bilanzanalyse, vol 9. Edition S + W, Hamburg

Schweitzer M et al (2016) Systeme der Kosten- und Erlösrechnung, 11th edn. Vahlen, München

Simons R (1995) Control in an age of empowerment. Harv Bus Rev 73(2):80–88

Speckbacher G, Bischof J, Pfeiffer T (2003) A descriptive analysis on the implementation of balanced scorecards in German-speaking countries. Manag Account Res 14(4):361–387

Trapp R (2012) Konvergenz des Rechnungswesens – eine Inhaltsanalyse der Diskussion um eine Annäherung des internen und externen Rechnungswesens in deutschsprachigen Fachzeitschriften. Gabler, Wiesbaden

Wall F (2001) Ursache-Wirkungsbeziehungen als ein zentraler Bestandteil der Balanced Scorecard Möglichkeiten und Grenzen ihrer Gewinnung. Controlling 13(2):65–74

Weber HK, Rogler S (2004) Bilanz sowie Gewinn- und Verlustrechnung, 5th edn. Betriebswirtschaftliches Rechnungswesen, vol 1. Vahlen, München

Weber J, Schäffer U (2020) Einführung in das Controlling, 16th edn. Schäffer-Poeschel, Stuttgart

Zünd A (1973) Kontrolle und Revision in der multinationalen Unternehmung. Haupt, Bern

The Steering Function of Controlling

Contents

S. Behringer, *Financial Controlling*,
https://doi.org/10.1007/978-3-658-40527-4_3

3

Learning Agenda

The steering function of financial controlling tries to control the behavior of employees and to coordinate it across the entire company. The central instrument for this is planning, which is also the basis for the control function, i.e. the comparison of target and actual values. This allows controlling to check whether the company is on the right track or whether measures to correct it are necessary. Planning poses many challenges: How should the planning be designed, who should be involved in its creation and how can one ensure that the planning participants do not abuse their information. The danger of distortion lies in the connection to the determination of variable compensation. Particular attention is paid to the derivation of goals in planning. The company must decide in which direction it wants to go. The statement "the company must ..." already shows the first problem: Who sets the goals? The abstract unit "company" cannot do this. People have to act for the company. Afterwards the question arises which target variables are relevant and how the target level is determined concretely.

Concept of planning	What does planning mean? What does a planning process look like? Which elements should a planning at least contain?	► Sect. 3.1
Functions and risks of planning	Which functions does planning take on? What risks arise from this?	► Sect. 3.2
Goals as the basis of planning	What are goals? How do you derive a good goal? What are possible goal sizes? What goals do companies set themselves in practice?	► Sect. 3.3
Course of planning	What role does management play in planning? What role does controlling play? Which departments are involved in the planning process in what way?	► Sect. 3.4
Incentive problems through planning	Which problems arise through the connection of incentives and planning? How can these problems be solved?	► Sect. 3.5
Alternative planning approaches	What alternatives are there to the established planning methods?	► Sect. 3.6

3.1 Concept of Planning

Planning is a core element of many business disciplines. One speaks of marketing planning, production planning or financial planning. The starting point of a planning is the existence of a system, i.e. a set of elements that are related to each other. Such a system is, for example, a medium-sized company that is organized as a sole proprietorship, or a large corporation that consists of many different legal and organizational units. The starting point of planning is that the state of this system is perceived by a person (this can be the planner himself, his superior, the manager or the owner) as unsatisfactory or improvable or, due to external claims, as no longer appropriate. Consequently, there is a difference between the current or future expected state and the desired future state described by goals (cf. Klein and Scholl 2004, p. 1). The planning is supposed to help by deriving fields of action to transfer the state of the status quo into the desired state. Planning is "prospective thinking" with the "future action" to be anticipated (Kosiol 1967, p. 79).

> In a nutshell: Planning is concerned with the design of the actions that are necessary to move from the current, non-optimal, state to the desired state. As such, it is a core component of the steering function.

From these considerations it follows that one can only plan those things that one can influence through actions. It is illogical to plan things that are predetermined from the outside. So you can't plan the weather. You have to accept it as given. The term **projection** is used for this. However, forecasts and plans are closely related. Data that influence the planning are projected. For example, external factors such as customer behavior, market developments, economic trends such as economic growth, inflation or salary developments should be forecasted because they have an impact on corporate planning.

Planning takes place for both operational and strategic purposes. Strategic planning has a time horizon of three to five years. The need to take into account events that are far into the future results from the fact that events in the future influence the success of today's entrepreneurial measures. Strategic corporate planning tries to get a handle on the uncertainty associated with this fact through prospective thinking (Albach 1968, p. 3). Operational planning concretizes the strategic corporate planning. It is its "executive instrument" (Schreyögg and Koch 2010, p. 138). The time horizon of operational planning is much shorter. As a rule, one year is considered

3

the maximum of the operational planning horizon. However, in some cases the operational planning horizon is also much shorter: For example, a cash planning, in which financial resources and due liabilities are to be covered, is made over a day; production planning can sometimes only have a horizon of a few hours (e.g. the scheduling in a service company). Strategic and operational planning often have quantities, lengths or time periods as their primary object. These sizes are transformed into money sizes with prices, so that financial planning results. Its purpose is to plan the result of the company, but on the other hand also to ensure the sufficient provision of the company with means of payment (liquidity). For this it is important to know which payment obligations will arise in the future for the company. This is achieved through planning. The creation of strategic and operational planning and financial planning overlap and interact with each other. If at first a strategic plan, then an operational plan and finally the financial planning is thought, this procedure is often different in practice. The operational planning requires strategic measures. Financial planning is not only a result of strategic and operational planning, it also makes specifications, as financial resources are often the bottleneck for strategic and operational measures.

Compared to improvised, i.e. unplanned decisions, one expects significant advantages from systematic planning. Planning helps to avoid wrong decisions, creates possibilities for control through the specification of goals and, through coordination and goal orientation, increases the chances of success of the enterprise. Plans bind those implementing them by specifying goals; but not—as in the coordination through fixed programs—with regard to the details of the process to achieve the goal.

Business studies have long been concerned with the question of whether planning has a positive effect on the result of a company or not. In a meta-study of 18 studies, Miller and Cardinal (1994) found a positive relationship between planning activities and the result of the company, even in turbulent environments, where one could actually expect a negative rigidity of the planning requirements. In a repetition of the meta-analysis from 2015, Cardinal et al. (2015) confirm the result of the positive relationship between planning and company success in principle, but also point out numerous content-related irregularities. For example, plans in emerging markets have a lower success effect than in established economies. Also, results differentiated by sector often have different implications.

Planning can be divided into the phases shown in ◘ Fig. 3.1 in thought. However, the individual phases are often not carried out strictly one after the other in business reality. Often, the planning phases run in parallel.

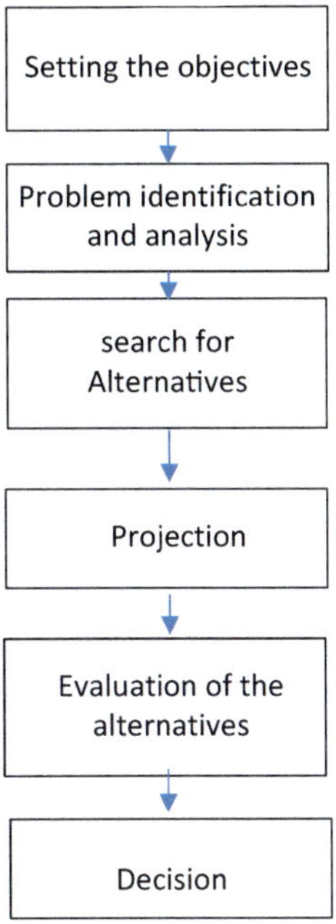

Fig. 3.1 Phases of the planning process. (Own illustration based on Küpper et al. 2013, p. 132)

The planning process begins with the **goal setting**. Starting from the strategic goals, these are broken down into operational goals. The operational goals must be such that they support the achievement of the strategic goals. The goals must be operational, essentially measurable. A measurable goal is, for example, to achieve an increase in profit over the previous year by 10%. An unsuitable goal, because it is not measurable, would be the formulation "to increase the profit significantly". Usually several goals are set. So it can be in the interest of a company to increase market share and profit. These two goals are not necessarily completely compatible with each other. The expansion of market shares can be in conflict with the goal of profit, for example because a low-price strategy can lead to an increase in market share. For such constellations, the relative importance of the goals must be specified, that is, how important an expansion of the market by x% is in relation to an increase in profit of Y euros.

The actual planning process is triggered by the identification of a problem. A state is perceived as unsatisfactory. The **problem analysis** investigates in what this dissatisfaction is based. For operational controlling processes, it is common for the dissatisfaction to be caused by the previous target-actual comparison (see ▶ Chap. 4), in which a deviation from previous planning specifications is detected. The planned profit is not achieved, measures must be taken to improve this situation. This triggers a new planning process.

Problem analysis is often accompanied by a first search for solutions. By concretizing the possible actions, alternatives arise from this. The effects of an alternative are shown in the forecast—what happens if this alternative is chosen. At the end of the planning process is the evaluation of the alternative. The evaluation takes into account the achievement of the goals set at the beginning. In the context of the decision, the best alternative should then be chosen.

A plan usually includes the following components (see Wild 1974, p. 49):

- Problem statement
- Planning goals
- Projected effects
- Available resources (financial, personnel or material resources for solving the problem)
- Individual measures and combination of individual measures into a package of measures
- Planning authority and planning responsible
- Time conditions and deadlines
- Assumptions and premises
- Information on connections to other plans.

In practice, not all corporate plans explicitly contain all of these elements. However, they are implicitly present in most plans at least to some extent (for example, as an assumed but not mentioned assumption). The basic task is to move from an initial state to a target state.

Problems that can be represented by planning can be both very significant and extensive or small. In the latter case, planning often takes place only in the head of the planning employee without being formally documented. Examples of problems are:

- Decision on founding a company
- Decision on the amount and timing of a price increase
- Shift schedule for the employees of a department
- Planning of the necessary funds to be raised from banks etc.

The examples make it clear that not only in financial controlling companies plan. Planning takes place in all departments of a company. Controlling is responsible for the overall company plan, in which the individual sub-plans (personnel, marketing, production plan, etc.) are converted into financial figures. At the end of corporate planning is a planned annual financial statement. Corporate planning, as we understand it here, is therefore a financial planning, but based on other quantitative variables (quantities, times, etc.).

Planning carriers are controlling and management together, each taking different roles. Controlling has the core task of securing the rationality of management. Planning and the control of corporate units based on it play an important role. Planning is therefore also a core task of controlling. However, decisions on the contents of the plan must be made by management, so that it must be clear which planning tasks are carried out by controlling and which planning tasks the management has to take over.

The actual planning, i.e. the factual and technical design of the plan, lies with the management. The controller essentially takes over the tasks of planning support and planning management. The controller will usually transfer the management's factual ideas into a plan, i.e. the qualitative specifications will be translated into monetary values by the controller. It is also the task of a controller to question the made premises and to check their reliability. In addition, during the process of creating the plan, controllers are expected to make preliminary arrangements. The often theoretically existing image of an isolated plan is particularly unreal in the case of complex or large companies. The interests and ideas of individual parts of the company go into the planning process. The individual sub-plans must build on each other and fit together. It is the task of the controller to prepare this and to coordinate it as far as possible (cf. Weber and Schäffer 2020, p. 269).

Remember!

The **plan** content is the responsibility of management. Controllers support this, in particular by taking over the planning management.

In practice, financial controlling takes over the function of organizing the planning. Controllers provide files or systems through which the planning is carried out. They set and monitor deadlines for submission, revision and decision of the plans. They advise the operational and strategic management in the preparation of the plans, answer their questions and secure the coordination and orientation on the overall goal of the company of the plan contents accompanying the preparation of the plan. If the first draft of the plan is available, the controlling department puts together the overall plan, carries out a first plausibility check, which may lead to changes in the departments, and creates the presentation templates for the top management. In many companies, the head of financial controlling also presents the first draft of the planning, whereby the controller should not appear here as responsible for the plan content, but as a messenger and interpreter of the planning.

3

3.2 Functions and Risks of Planning

Planning plays several important roles in companies, which are also clearly visible in the time spans related to planning by controllers and managers (cf. Weber et al. 2009, pp. 90 ff.). Both groups use a large part of their working time on the planning process. Management is also willing to deal extensively with planning issues, which suggests the importance of the planning process. In concrete terms, planning takes over the following functions (cf. Steinmann and Schreyögg 2005, pp. 333 ff.):

- You think about future achievable results. Management is forced to derive precise actions for the future expressed in monetary values. This gives management a stronger **future orientation** and can react earlier to changing environmental conditions. This is important to keep the company competitive in the long term and sustainable. Many developments that have an impact on the company are not immediately recognizable. For a long time, it was unthinkable for companies in the photography industry to get their main competition from manufacturers in the telecommunications sector. Many manufacturers of photos were surprised by the development of photo functions on mobile phones. If you take the time to think systematically about future developments, you increase the likelihood of recognizing relevant trends. Planning thus becomes an **early warning system** for the company. You recognize risks during planning that could endanger the future economic situation.
- Planning leads to a **coordination** of all activities in the company. All company departments are forced to talk to each other and coordinate their sub-plans during the annual planning process. Centralized financial controlling has the opportunity to coordinate the sub-departments and prevent uncoordinated, ineffective action. One can imagine what uncoordinated activities can trigger in terms of damage. For example, if the marketing department promotes a product line that is taken off the

production line, there is economic damage due to wasted resources, but there is also probably a loss of reputation, as customers are unhappy when they can no longer buy the desired products that they know from advertising. The coordination function of planning was also responsible for the establishment of the controller function in companies. The first controller positions were set up in American companies after the complexity increased due to the size of the company and consequently the coordination became necessary (cf. Stoffel 1995, p. 8). This is also reflected in an empirical observation: The larger a company is, the more controller positions there are (cf. Küpper et al. 2013, p. 668). However, it should not be neglected that larger controlling departments have to coordinate more with each other. Once the first phase of the planning process is over, the controller has to check the first draft of the plan for consistency. It must finally be determined whether the individual assumptions actually fit together. The starting point for this examination is the bottleneck, that is, the situation that limits the entire company and its development. In a market economy, this is usually sales. In principle, a large amount can be produced, customers determine through their demand how much is actually sold and thus also produced sensibly. However, it is also conceivable that procurement or production is the limiting factor, e.g. the purchase of a raw material. For a while, the procurement of silicon was the bottleneck in the production of solar cells. However, in general, the planning must be sales-oriented. The fact that all subplans must be coordinated with the minimum sector is referred to as the **compensation law of planning** (cf. Gutenberg 1983, pp. 163 ff.). This also means that as soon as a planning assumption changes with regard to the bottleneck, the whole planning process has to start all over again

- Closely linked to coordination is the **promotion of communication**. The individual company parts are forced to talk to each other and exchange information. This gives the central management, but also the individual departments themselves, the opportunity to identify bottlenecks that require special attention, e.g. by investments. Planning provides the stage in practice for the comprehensive discussion of all business-relevant issues in the company. It therefore has the function of a general debate—depending on the design of the planning system only from top to bottom or also from bottom to top—analogous to the budget debate in politics. Planning thus leads to the fact that the individual departments talk to each other and develop ideas together on how to meet the challenges of the future.

- Not to be underestimated is the importance of planning as a benchmark for managers. Planning has a **prescriptive function** and thus provides employees at all levels of hierarchy with information about which contributions to corporate success are expected from them. Deviations from the budget upwards can be associated with rewards, e.g. B. by linking income or part of income to the achievement of budget targets. Deviations from the budget downwards can be associated with sanctions, on the other hand. This is particularly the case when **variable compensation** is fixed. Studies show that CEOs and other executives receive the vast majority of their compensation in variable form. The actual payment of the compensation is made dependent on the achievement of the plan. As will be shown later, this gives the planning a partly problematic double function. While the coordination and communication function of planning, like the future-oriented expression it expresses, bring creative and constructive aspects with them, the compensation function tempts to set the benchmark so low that it is easily achieved and thus easy to achieve increased compensation. Another purpose of planning in this context is to inform employees: As part of their participation in the planning, they learn about the restrictions, deadlines or decisions.

Remember!

The essential **planning functions** are thinking about the future, coordinating decentralized activities within a company, promoting communication within the company and the motivational function by setting goals for employees at different levels of hierarchy.

In addition to the already mentioned danger that plans can no longer fulfil their creative, future-oriented functions properly through the mixture with the assessment of variable compensation, the danger also arises of too pronounced a budget mentality, as is often the case, for example, in the public sector. The budget must be fulfilled exactly. Opportunities for over-fulfilment are missed because this could have negative (too high future targets) consequences for future target setting. In addition, a rigid adherence to plans can lead to wrong decisions. After plan creation, the framework conditions for entrepreneurial action may have changed so that an action according to the plan is no longer appropriate. Too rigid adherence to plans or blind faith in planning can lead to inflexibility.

Another problem area is the great complexity of companies. The idea of planning all developments and thus controlling the future inevitably fails because of the difficulty of capturing all influencing factors on entrepreneurial decisions. The complexity also makes coordination more difficult. Planning all factors simultaneously in the sense of a comprehensive corporate planning no longer fails due to the lack of or expensive computer capacities, but rather because of the difficulty of modelling the entire company in its context. Therefore, the individual departments of the company are planned successively. This has the consequence that not all interdependencies in the company can be recognized. For example, the departure of a certain employee in the field of research and development can lead to delays in the market launch of a product. This reduces the achievable sales and thus the profit. This situation is probably not anticipatable in a planning process. Closely related to this argument is the uncertainty of the forecast. The theoretical assumption that the consequences of the choice of an alternative can be predicted exactly is not realistic. In the real world, there are decision-making situations under risk—the occurrence of the consequences of action is known with probabilities—or even uncertainty—the probabilities of the occurrence of certain consequences of action are unknown. Due to the uncertainty, the aim of planning is not to predict the consequences of action as accurately as possible. Planning serves rather the preparation of decisions and should ensure that decisions are made on a solid basis and that the consequences of chosen actions are not overestimated or underestimated.

Business administration has developed planning instruments that are intended to help carry out the planning in a targeted manner so that the risks of planning do not occur.

3.3 Goals as the Basis of Planning

3.3.1 Goal Setting

Goals are desirable future states. They relate to the future and indicate how the current status quo should change. They take the form of imperatives. Imperative is the linguistic imperative form or, in other words, the request to do or not do certain actions. This is the difference between the wish, the goal expresses a stronger need for action. A business goal does not refer to a single action but to a bundle of actions. Consequently, business goals can be represented as "general imperatives" for example "Seek profit!" (Heinen 1971, p. 51).

In business administration, profit maximization is often postulated as a goal for companies. But the problem with this goal is that there are different groups of stakeholders who want to achieve goals with a company. There is no abstract company goal. People have goals, organizations do not (Cyert and March 1995, p. 29). The goals that **stakeholder groups** want to achieve in and with a company can vary or even conflict with each other. So employees strive for high salaries, customers for low prices and high quality. Both goals are in conflict with each other, because one euro less sales price also means one euro less for salaries.

Since there are different stakeholders who have a legitimate interest in the company, it is questionable which group sets the goals to which the members of the organization feel obliged. In practice, it is usually the top management that suggests the goals. This proposal is then confirmed or changed by the owners, represented by the supervisory board in public companies (in which employees are also represented in larger companies in Germany). So in practice, there are usually two stakeholders who are explicitly involved in goal setting: management and owners. All other internal stakeholders are fixed on these goals by the different incentive systems. However, employees and other stakeholders can still try to achieve their own goals within the company. The official goal of profit maximization will not prevent an employee from continuing to try to maximize his personal income with low workload.

Goals take different dimensions and have different aspects. **Formal goals** are financial goals (e.g. profit goals or increase in company value). This is to be distinguished from the **material goals**. They describe the performance-oriented goals, for example to build an excellent car. An investor is more interested in the formal goal whether he is dealing with a car company or an electrical company, is usually secondary.

Another distinction concerns **basic, strategic and operational goals**. Basic goals are fundamental for the entire company. They stand above all other goals. They are not explicitly formulated in many companies, but there is tacit agreement among all company employees that this goal exists. The most important thing is the existence of the company. In particular, in the Mittelstand, but also in larger companies, the independence of the company is also to be secured.

The explicit goals of a company are distinguished by their validity. In the literature, the image of the pyramid has proven to be useful for this purpose (cf. ◘ Fig. 3.2).

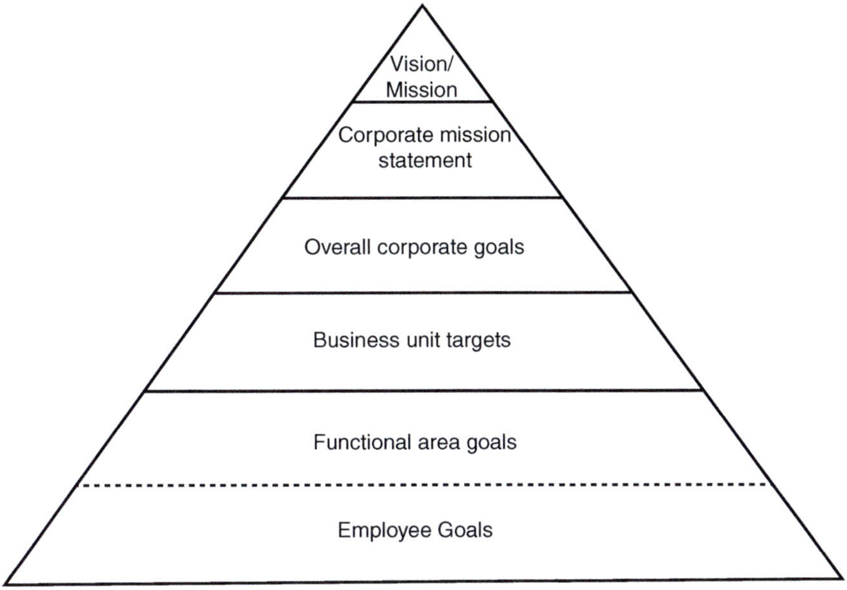

Fig. 3.2 Target pyramid. (Own representation based on Jung et al. 2016, p. 142)

The **vision and mission** or the corporate identity of the company contains basic statements that apply to all stakeholders. They are valid in the long term and embody the DNA of the company. The mission contains the purpose of the company. It answers the question "What is our business?". This is where the purpose of the company is represented. The basic material goal is formulated. The company should work out its core competence and its unique selling point here. Normally, missions are very stable and rarely changed.

The vision answers the question "What do we want to become?". The vision should be oriented towards the future on the one hand, but on the other hand, it should encompass a period of time in which the feasibility of future prospects is still foreseeable. Normally, a period of 5 to 10 years is assumed.

▶ Example: Vision

The vision of the Swedish furniture store Ikea is generally considered to be very successful. Ikea states its vision on its homepage: "To create a better everyday life for the many people". ◀

The vision and mission are concretized in the **corporate identity**. In addition, the basic values that the company wants to embody are laid down here. With the corporate identity, the identification of all stakeholders should also be aroused. Therefore, positive emotions are often used.

Both mission, vision and corporate identity are not the direct subject of financial controlling but the framework conditions of their actions. All three also have in common that they are often not measurable in a concrete way. From the theory of strategic management, all three elements are seen as a standard of good management. However, their usefulness in practice is limited, especially if they were created without the involvement of employees (Müller-Stewens and Lechner 2011, p. 232).

This sets the framework for further goal setting. The overall corporate goals break down the very long-term specifications of the vision into operationalized sub-goals. These sub-goals serve to bring the company closer to the desired goal of the vision. Here, goals should then be formulated so that they are **SMART**. With the acronym SMART, it is meant that a goal should meet the following criteria:

- Specific: Goals should be formulated unambiguously and clearly.
- Measurable: There should be a clear and comprehensible operationalization.
- Demanding: A high goal should be chosen.
- Realistic: Despite high ambitions, the goal should be achievable.
- Timelines: There should be a clear time reference, i.e. it should answer when it should be achieved.

▶ Example: Goal that meets the SMART method

The product XY will generate sales of 1,000,000 € in the 2022 financial year. The goal is specific (no doubt about the content, as sales is a well-defined size), measurable (sales volume is given) and the time reference is given (2022 financial year). It is ambitious if sales are increased compared to the previous year. It is realistic if the increase appears to be realizable on the market. ◀

The method goes back to the **Goal-Setting Theory** and in particular to Locke and Latham (1984). They wanted to set themselves apart from the

"Do your best" goals that were often used by companies. These gave the employee the goal of achieving the best possible result and thus violated all the rules of the SMART technique.

The company's overall goals are then broken down further, first to the business areas, then to the functional areas (production, marketing, sales, etc.), and finally to the individual employee.

Ideally, this process runs chronologically in a company. The goals of the higher level of the pyramid are distributed to the lower level. This results in a consistent picture in which the target sizes can be added up from bottom to top. In practice, this ideal picture is often violated. Especially at the very top, changes keep happening that are not passed on to the lower levels. Reasons for this can be, for example, requirements from investors who expect high profits. They express this at a time when most of the employees have already been talked to. Hardly any company will adjust the functional area or employee goals in this situation, but leave them where they were once set.

To formulate goals correctly, it is helpful to answer the two following questions (cf. Ulrich and Probst 1995, pp. 122 f.):

1. Does the goal to be discussed correspond to the higher-level goals on the pyramid? Would these goals also allow for another target setting?
2. Is it realistic to achieve the goal under discussion? How will expected changes in the conditions affect the achievability of the goal? Does the current or future situation require a change in our target setting?

Goals can stand in different relationships to each other. There are **complementary goals**, in which the achievement of both goals promotes each other. As a rule, for example, the desired increase in sales leads to an increase in profits. With **competing goals**, the two goals mutually hinder each other. So the goal of cost reduction is in tension with the increase in market share. A classic case of goal competition is the relationship between liquidity and profitability. An extreme case is the **goal antinomy**, in which the achievement of a goal is only possible by giving up the achievement of another goal. There are often **indifferent goals**, in which the manifestations of the two target variables have no mutual effects.

In the case of competing goals, it must be decided which goal has priority or how the weights are to be distributed among the various goals.

3.3.2 Empirical Findings on Goal Setting in Companies

Empirical goal research has a long tradition. However, it is based on methodologically difficult grounds, since the goals are mostly gained by means of surveys, without plausibilizing them with the actual company behavior. Therefore, it cannot be ruled out with all findings that the answers of the companies are shaped by social desirability.

In the 1960s and 1970s, researchers were able to identify a dominance of the profit goal in empirical studies (cf. Macharzina and Wolf 2017, p. 230). In the 1980s, the securing of competitiveness was identified as the dominant goal. The maximization of profits took a back seat, supplemented by ecological and social goals.

With the appearance of books on **Shareholder Value**, this corporate goal has spread widely. Pioneer companies such as General Electric or in Germany VEBA AG (today E.on) were the first to introduce this principle. Empirical studies around the turn of the millennium then also show the advance of shareholder value as a goal.

Likewise, there is a further increased focus on goals with ecological and social content. However, it is questionable whether these goals are not chosen because they also increase profits or corporate value at least indirectly, as more customers want to purchase ecologically correct products, and there are ethically oriented investors who increase the demand for a company's shares.

3.3.3 Examples of Goals

3.3.3.1 Shareholder Value as a Corporate Goal

In the 1980s, the shareholder value idea gradually established itself as the prevailing paradigm for the objectives of managers and companies. The idea is based on introduced concepts that have been combined into a new approach. The approaches come from financial theory, corporate valuation, controlling and strategic management. The aim of the shareholder value concept is to make different objectives of owners (shareholders) and managers compatible. The shareholders are interested in rising stock prices and high dividends. The managers often have an interest in conflict, as they want to achieve higher salaries. If the management decisions and thus also the variable compensation are linked to the effects of the decision consequences on the enterprise value, the two areas can be made compatible with each other. Managers are afraid of losing their jobs. The small shareholder is not able to check whether the management is working in his interest or not. But the capital market can do this very well: The share price development of the shares is a daily judgment about the performance of the management. If the price is too low, the company represents an easy target for purchases by other investors. These investors will often want to replace the management, as the previous price development has spoken a negative judgment about the performance of the management. If the management—analogous to the objectives of the shareholders—strives for high prices, this danger is obviated.

Remember!

The **Shareholder Value** can be defined (for listed companies) as: Shareholder Value = Enterprise Value = Number of shares · Share price of a share.

It is immediately clear that with this success criterion, the objectives of managers and owners are aligned. But this principle can also be applied sensibly to family businesses, which in Germany and Switzerland contribute a large part of the economic performance. Families usually have all their assets or a large part of their assets tied up in their business. The long-term value development is of particular importance to the family, as they may have to finance their further livelihood from the sale of the company in doubt. The shareholder value is therefore misleading in that it does not only refer to stock values and shares. In general, one could translate it with owner value. However, for non-listed companies, the stock market listing is missing, through which a market value is determined every day. For non-listed companies, the value must therefore be determined analytically.

This analytical approach is mostly determined by the **total capital approach** in practice. The value results according to the following:

$$\text{Total value of the company} = \sum \frac{FCF_t}{(1 + WACC)^t}$$

The **Free Cashflow (FCF)** of an entire company or the company's division is discounted at the weighted average cost of capital (Weighted Average Cost of Capital, WACC). **Cashflow** refers to the payment balances, that is, the deposits minus the withdrawals. Deposits and withdrawals refer to changes in liquid assets, which consist of cash and daily due bank balances. An example of a withdrawal is the cash payment of a bill. An example of a deposit is the cash sale to a customer. The cash flow reflects the cash surplus generated by a company or reporting unit in a period and essentially provides a key figure for assessing the financial and liquidity situation, which in addition indicates the internal financing volume generated by the company. The free cash flow refers to those cash surpluses that remain after investments and financing costs, that is, after the external capital providers have received their interest. After the company has made all the necessary investments, the free cash flow is what remains and is available for distributions to the owners.

▶ Example: Derivation of the free cash flow of Kitty Fitness GmbH

Kitty Fitness GmbH made a profit of 100,000 € before taxes at the end of the year. To get to the free cash flow, the following items have to be corrected:

	Annual surplus	**100,000**
+	Feed to the provisions	20,000
+	Depreciation	15,000
–	Investments	70,000
=	**Free Cashflow**	**65.000**

The annual surplus is to be corrected in the first step by the accrual of provisions. These are to be added because they have already reduced the annual surplus, but have not yet led to any disbursements. Depreciation reflects the value consumption of an asset. The asset has already led to a payment at the time of its acquisition, but no further payment is made at the time of depreciation. Investments are not immediately reflected in the annual surplus (only through depreciation over the course of the useful life). But they lead directly to a payment. ◀

To determine the shareholder value, the free cash flows are determined according to the principle of asset conservation, i.e. necessary investments in the company's fixed and current assets are deducted. Necessary means that the company can be maintained in its current state through these investments.

The aim of the free cash flow is to calculate a total value for the company. For this reason, it does not contain any payments to the capital providers. Consequently, it is stated before interest, i.e. it is assumed that the company is purely self-financed. This assumption has the consequence that a total value for the company is calculated which shows the sum of equity and liabilities. For the owner, only the value of equity is relevant, so that the value of liabilities has to be deducted to determine the value of the company. This means that the free cash flow contains the funds that can be used to pay liabilities in the form of interest and repayments, and equity in the form of dividends.

In addition, the after-tax free cash flows are calculated. The taxes also have to take into account that full self-financing is assumed. Interest on equity reduces the tax burden because it is deducted as an expense in the income statement before taxes. As a rule, a period of 5 to 10 years is assumed for controlling purposes, within which the free cash flows are planned in detail. A residual value is added to the planned values, which reflects the future cash flows after the end of the planning period. The importance of this residual value is often underestimated. Depending on the length of the detailed forecast period and the interest rate used, the residual value can contribute more than half to the total value (cf. Behringer 2016, pp. 500 ff.). For external corporate analysts, only indirect determination of the cash flow is usually possible due to lack of information. They choose the indirect derivation of the cash flow, in which the annual surplus is corrected for non-payment-effective elements (cf. the example presented above).

The **free cash flow** is determined in two steps (cf. Brühl 2016, p. 393):

- In the first step, the operating cash flow (before interest and taxes) is calculated. This results in:
  - Operating cash flow (before interest and taxes) = operating receipts—operating payments.
- In the second step, one arrives at the free cash flow:
  - Free cash flow (before interest, dividends and repayment) = operating cash flow (before interest and taxes)—tax payments ± payment balance for replacement and expansion investments in property, plant and equipment for asset preservation ± payment balance for the increase / decrease in current assets for asset preservation.

The weighted average cost of capital WACC is used as a discount factor to determine the value of the company. Formally expressed as a return requirement for the valuation of the entire company, these are weighted as the cost of equity with the equity share and the cost of debt with the cost of debt. This return requirement results as follows (cf. Krag and Kasperzak 2000, pp. 87 ff.):

$$\mathrm{WACC} = k_{FK} \cdot \frac{FK}{GK} + k_{EK} \cdot \frac{EK}{GK}$$

Where:
FK – = Debt
EK – = Equity
GK – = Share capital
k – = Cost

3

Note!

The **weighted average cost of capital (WACC)** of a company represents the hurdle that an investment must clear in order to be worthwhile for the company. If the return on an investment is above the WACC, shareholder value is created. If the return on an investment is below the WACC, shareholder value is destroyed.

If you rearrange the above equation by solving for k_{EK} and replacing WACC with the equity cost of the unlevered company k_{EK}^{u}(this is the so-called **Modigliani-Miller adjustment**) you get:

$$k_{EK} = k_{EK}^{u} + \left(k_{EK}^{u} - k_{FK}\right) \cdot \frac{FK}{EK}$$

The return that owners of a leveraged company demand corresponds to the return demanded for an unlevered company plus a risk premium that corresponds to the difference between the equity cost of the unlevered company minus interest on debt (assuming the interest on debt is less than the equity cost of the unlevered company) multiplied by the debt ratio of the leveraged company. This follows the intuitive logic that leveraged companies must generate higher returns because they are more risky than companies without leverage.

In order to determine the discounting factor WACC, one must determine the equity and debt costs. The current claims of the creditors on the company can be easily determined by means of a company analysis, since the creditors usually receive contractually specified consideration for the provision of capital in the form of interest (cf. Helbling 1993, p. 160). This does not apply to provisions, which have a high proportion in the balance sheets of most companies. Provisions refer to uncertain liabilities, special practical relevance have the provisions for occupational pension. The claim is acquired by the employee when he is still employed. Neither the time of retirement nor the life expectancy is known, so that it is clearly about uncertain liabilities. These liabilities are interest-bearing. So they are also shown in the balance sheet, as they, like other long-term liabilities, are discounted, i.e. discounted, in the balance sheet (cf. Behringer 2012, pp. 945 ff.).

Much more problematic is the estimation of the cost of equity, since the equity providers do not receive any contractually specified revenues in return for the provision of capital, but the residue, i.e. the result which, in the best case, remains after deduction of all expenses. Theoretically, the approach of the return of the optimal alternative to the investment in the company—i.e. the opportunity costs according to the best displaced alternative through the purchase of shares—would be correct. The derivation of these costs is practically not feasible, since there is an infinite number of available alternatives. You can invest in a study, buy other shares or buy gold. In financial controlling, therefore, a roughly simplified solution is usually sought, which is based on capital market theory and in particular on the **Capital Asset Pricing Model (CAPM)**. The question arises as to what return could be achieved with an investment in a security (other possible investments are excluded), with the same risk. Rational investors have, according to the CAPM, an expected return r_{EK} on a security, which is composed of the risk-free interest rate i* and a risk premium RP:

$$r_{EK} = i^* + RP$$

The investor is therefore risk-averse: a higher return is demanded for payments which are subject to greater uncertainty. This corresponds to the Modigliani-Miller adaptation presented above.

The risk premium results on the one hand from the risk premium which is due on investments in a risky market portfolio. This corresponds to the difference between the expected return of the market portfolio r_M and the risk-free interest rate i*. In addition to the **unsystematic risk**, which arises solely through investment in the risky market portfolio and is not compensated for in the market equilibrium, the **systematic risk** is of importance, which denotes the relation of the price development of the investment under consideration to the development of the market portfolio. This is calculated by the CAPM through the **β-factor**. The β-factor is the measure of the sensitivity between the expected return of the individual security and the expected return of the market portfolio. It shows the relative volatility of a security compared to another security or index.

If the β-factor of investment j is multiplied by the risk premium for investment in the risky market portfolio, the risk premium which a rational investor will demand for a certain security j results (cf. Ballwieser 1995, p. 122):

$$r_{EK} = i^* + \beta_j \cdot (r_M - i^*)$$

In addition to the cost of equity, the company must achieve at least this equity return. If more than this minimum return is earned, the company creates value, that is, it generates more than the owners require. The minimum return requirement of the owners must be paid out. If the company is able to generate additional profits, this is shown theoretically in an increasing company value, that is, an increasing stock price for the publicly traded company. However, this is only a theoretical assumption, as stock prices are subject to various influences and cannot be predicted by theoretical models.

▶ Example: Calculating WACC for Kitty Fitness GmbH

The controlling of Kitty Fitness GmbH would like to calculate the WACC of their company. The controllers have the following information available for this:

- Yield of risk-free investments 6.0%
- Yield of market portfolio 12.0%
- β-factor 0.8
- Interest rate for equity 8.0%
- Equity share 40%
- Income tax rate 30%

The WACC should be considered after taxes.

In the first step, the controllers represent the equity costs. They result from the following formula:

$$r_{EK} = i^* + \beta_j (r_M - i^*)$$

By substituting the data given above, the following result is obtained:

$$r_{EK} = 6{,}0 + 0{,}8(12{,}0 - 6{,}0) = 6{,}0 + 4{,}8 = 10{,}8$$

The equity capital costs of Kitty Fitness GmbH therefore amount to 10.8%. The required return from the perspective of the owners corresponds to the costs of equity from the perspective of the company. In this respect, it applies that r_{EK} is equal to k_{EK}. The cost of debt is given at 8.0%. However, there is now a significant difference between equity and debt costs. The equity investors are served from the profit after taxes. The cost of debt, on the other hand, can be deducted from taxes. They have a tax advantage over equity costs. In order to make both types of capital costs comparable, only the rate after taxes is taken into account at the cost of debt. The cost of debt is multiplied by (1- tax rate) to make equity and debt costs comparable:

$$k_{FK} = (1 - \text{Tax rate}) \cdot 8{,}0 = (1 - 30\%) \cdot 8{,}0 = 5{,}6$$

The cost of debt after taxes is therefore 5.6%.
With the information that the equity share is 40%, the share of debt can be calculated. It automatically results that the share of debt is 60%. Now the WACC can be calculated:

$$\begin{aligned} WACC = k_{FK} \cdot \tfrac{FK}{GK} + k_{EK} \cdot \tfrac{EK}{GK} &= 5{,}6 \cdot 60\% + 10{,}8 \cdot 40\% \\ &= 3{,}36 + 4{,}32 = 7{,}68 \end{aligned}$$

The WACC is 7.68%. They can be used as a discounting factor for the determination of the enterprise value. Furthermore, they can be used to function as a hurdle for investments. An investment then creates value if it generates a return of more than 7.68% of the capital invested. Only then are the claims of the owners covered. Anything above a return of 7.68% increases the enterprise value. Consequently, only investments should be made that generate a higher return than 7.68% of the invested capital. ◀

The consideration of the return requirements of the equity investors is fundamental for the shareholder value orientation of corporate management. In the traditional profit-oriented view, equity investors receive the amount that remains after deducting all expenses. When making investment decisions in value-oriented controlling, the cost of equity is already priced in. This increases the hurdle for successful investments. On the other hand, the goals of the owners can be directly taken into account in all entrepreneurial decisions. Shareholder value is by its nature a long-term goal of corporate management. However, this goal has become self-employed in practice and in public perception and has become detached from its original meaning: It is mostly associated with short-term price increases.

3.3.3.2 Stakeholder Value as Corporate Goal

If a company is run with the goal of increasing shareholder value, only two stakeholder groups are taken into account in goal setting: the owners and the management. Of course, there are more stakeholder groups that have a legitimate interest in participating in the company's goal setting. Think of employees outside of management, but also creditors, suppliers, or the general public. The goal of the stakeholder value approach for setting goals within the company is to take these groups into account. The followers of stakeholder value are of the opinion that it is incomprehensible to only involve two stakeholder groups in goal setting. The various stakeholders form a coalition with the goal of increasing the common wealth through the company. Shareholders have a legitimate interest in dividends and share price increases. However, this legitimate interest must be related to the legitimate interests of other stakeholders.

The problem with this idea is that the interests of the stakeholders are partly in conflict with each other. So employees want secure jobs and high pay. This is in contradiction to the profit-seeking of shareholders. The demand that managers of a company take these relationships into account and moderate them is easy to make (Clarkson 1995). However, the concrete quantification in a goal that meets the SMART criteria is almost impossible. Therefore, stakeholder orientation is usually only formulated as a soft qualitative goal. As a rule, it therefore also does not find direct entry into the controlling reports.

3.3.4 Derivation of the Target Value

So far, we have discussed the meaningful target variables in this chapter. But this does not yet determine how high the target should be determined or which reference value is sensible. Four methods can be distinguished for determining the target value (cf. Weber and Schäffer 2020, pp. 71 ff.):

- **Past values**: The simplest method and probably the most widely used approach is the continuation of the values of the past. However, past values can be distorted by one-time effects, a large order may not be repeatable. In addition, a value achieved in the past is not necessarily a sign of great success. The first professor of business administration in Germany Eugen Schmalenbach formulated that if target variables are derived from the past, "laziness with laziness" (Schmalenbach 1934, p. 263) is compared.
- Logically, the derivation of objectives would be based on forecasts that process the information available in the company about the development of target variables. The prerequisite is that all available information is truthfully and completely disclosed. In practice, this approach is often chosen despite the expected difficulties. Forecasts are also based on the past, but they include information about the future. However, they are all implicitly based on the assumption that the regularities of the past can be continued. This approach will certainly be strengthened in the near future by digital innovations such as predictive analytics (cf. ▸ Sect. 5.1).

- Comparative values (benchmarks): **Benchmarking** is a systematic comparison between companies of a certain class (size, regional location, industry, etc.). The aim is to learn from the comparison in order to become the benchmark itself, that is, the best. By comparing with external competitors, an ambitious but realistic goal can be determined. However, a mere comparison of figures may be too short-sighted. The purely quantitative comparison does not allow to recognize the causes based in processes that explain the different results. In this respect, one should carry out a more systematic benchmarking (cf. Nagel and Mieke 2014, pp. 248 ff.). While with an external benchmarking the problem exists to get to the data and the reasons for their manifestation, with internal benchmarking the problem is that one may compare "laziness with laziness" again. Nevertheless, in practice, internal benchmarking is carried out in many companies—especially if various subsidiaries perform similar tasks (e.g. the distribution of a centrally produced product) in different countries. In this case, a deviation from the best in the company can only be explained by local deviations. With external benchmarking, one can learn something beyond the mere target setting, provided that one wins the best performer as a partner. If one had a direct competitor, the findings could be transferred—in addition to the mere comparison of figures. A partner can be found more easily in the functional comparison. For example, two online retailers can compare their logistics activities and look for improvements together if they do not have the same products on offer. Benchmarking has a high relevance in controlling both in target setting and in initiating improvement processes, as studies among medium-sized companies (Krolak et al. 2011) and large listed companies (Schäffer and Weber 2015) show.
- **Normatively specified goals**: With normatively specified goals, the target level is set autonomously by the management without explicit reference to models from the past or competition. This goal setting always makes sense when there are no models, for example when a new area is being set up. So US President Kennedy had the vision of bringing people to the moon and back to Earth, which he did. Samsung wanted to be one of the ten leading manufacturers of automobiles by 2010 (Sull 2005, p. 5). This did not succeed. In addition, normative goal setting always makes sense when the other derivations lead to endless discussions. The goal-setting process can be shortened by normative goal setting.

Most companies combine the individual methods. Often, a goal is compiled from a mixture of past values and forecast values. Benchmarks are then included in this first derivation, which are rarely systematically collected. In the end, there is usually a normative specification that takes into account all other inputs.

3.4 Course of the Planning Process

The planning process is led by the financial controllers of a company. They are responsible for the smooth and effective design of the planning process. As a rule, a distinction is made between the plans that contribute to the material objectives of the company. Target variables are quantities, qualities or times—for example the number of wine bottles a winemaker produces. The other planning variables contribute to the formal goal. They can all be expressed in monetary values. For example, the revenue of a winery results from the number of bottles multiplied by their prices. Both planning variables are closely related. The turnover determines the possibilities to invest in marketing, successful marketing in turn leads to more turnover.

In the **master budget**, which is schematically shown in ◘ Fig. 3.3, planning of sales is usually started. In the market economy, sales are usually the bottleneck for further expansion. For this reason, the whole plan must relate to this bottleneck. The weakest area is practically the driving force for the other business areas. If the planned sales change, this results in changes in production planning, procurement, etc. So the law of planning applies. The driving force for everything else can also be the finance sector. If the liquid funds are lacking, this inhibits the investment activity of the company, which in turn reduces production possibilities and consequently sales opportunities.

In this respect, the planning process is theoretically a mathematical-analytical activity: From the specification of a planned target value for sales, the necessary production quantities and consequently the financial requirements for investments, staff recruitment, etc. result. Of course, this is only a theoretical approach. In practice, the planning is created by communication between different departments and hierarchy levels of the company, experience, political games and demonstrations of power. The concrete design depends on the overall situation of the company.

There are usually differences in the concrete design of the planning depending on the centralization of the planning process. Is the plan set from above (**top-down**) or do the lower hierarchy levels play a greater role (**bottom-up**)?

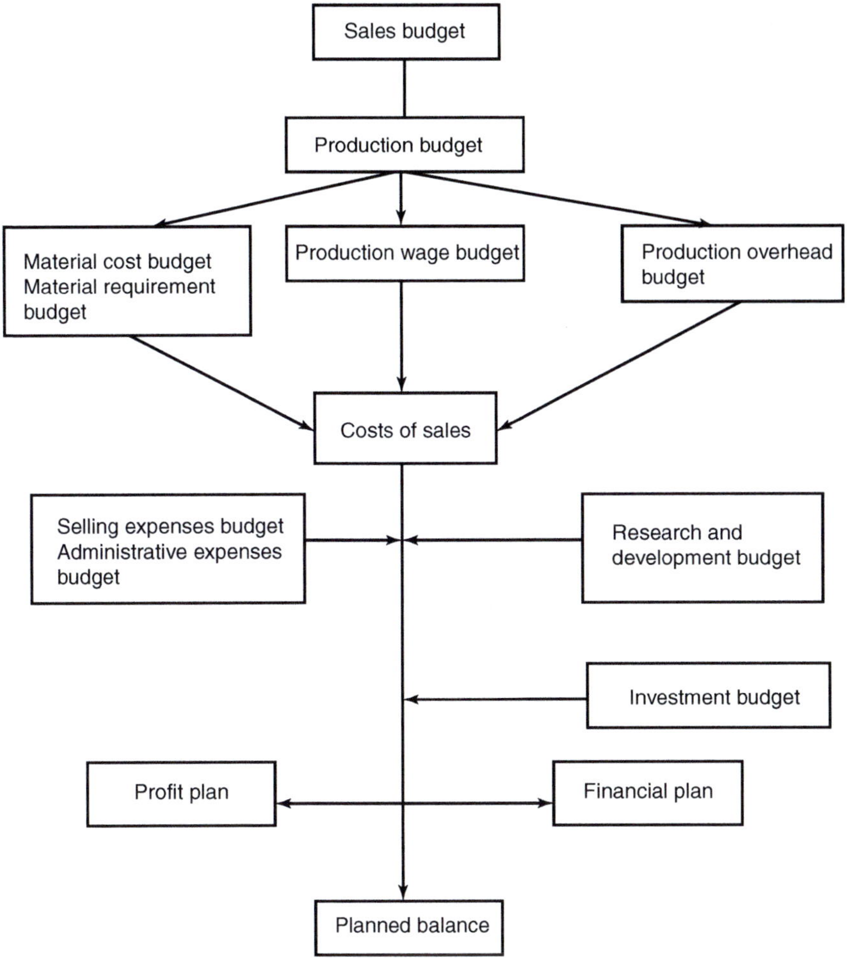

Fig. 3.3 Master budget. (Cf.Ewert and Wagenhofer 2014, p. 405)

In top-down planning (also called retrograde planning), the budget is established without the participation of decentralized management. This means that decentralized management essentially has its targets dictated by top management. This can only be effective if top management has planning-relevant knowledge. The decentralized planning that also takes place in departments serves only to specify and detail the targets. The problem arises when management overestimates its own planning-relevant

3

knowledge. This can lead to unrealistic budget figures that can trigger wrong decisions. In contrast, participation of decentralized management makes the knowledge of decentralized units part of the budgets. Furthermore, one can assume that participation increases one's own motivation. A dictated target does not lead to identification, as is the case with a target to which one has contributed to its formulation. In the top-down planning environment, the controller has more the function of a whip-cracker who, when transferring to decentralized budgets, must ensure that the target set by corporate management is also implemented. Pure top-down planning is a theoretical construct that will be so rarely encountered in practice.

The opposite extreme is called bottom-up planning (also called progressive planning). Decentralized management is asked for its assessment of the situation and future prospects. This assessment is adopted by management into the planning. Top management only has the function of coordinating the individual sub-plans. It is assumed that planning-relevant knowledge lies with decentralized units because they either have product or market knowledge. The role of the controller is to collect the individual plans and consolidate them into the company's overall plan. In doing so, the controller must ensure that the individual parts fit together. The bottom-up planning increases the coordination requirements significantly. In addition, there are many reasons why decentralized units may not disclose true information, e.g. because their salary is linked to target achievement.

Bottom-up and top-down planning are theoretical ideal images that are not used in most companies. Most companies (see Horváth et al. 1985, p. 147) use the **countercurrent method** (see ◘ Fig. 3.4) in practice, which tries

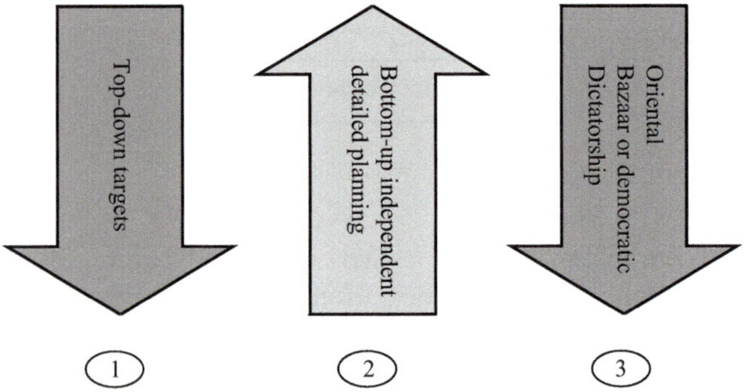

◘ **Fig. 3.4** Schematic representation of the countercurrent process. (Source: Behringer 2018, p. 145)

to combine the advantages of the two ideal images. The starting point is the idea that the planning-relevant knowledge is distributed across all hierarchical levels of the company. No level can create an efficient and effective budget on its own. The plan is determined iteratively in the countercurrent process. Budgeting takes place in at least three steps. First, the company management (roughly) sets the goals in the top-down process for the decentralized units. These serve as guidelines for the bottom-up planning of the decentralized units. The guideline is not to be understood as mandatory, but the decentralized units are asked to take into account their actual possibly also divergent assessments. These bottom-up plans are then compared with the specifications made by the top management at the beginning of the process. As a rule, the bottom-up figures will be less challenging than the top-down specifications. In a third phase, the two parts of the planning are then brought together. It is about how the gap between top-down specifications and bottom-up results can be divided. In this phase, negotiations can be used, which means that the decentralized units are more involved, which can degenerate into a kind of oriental bazaar with haggling. A second possibility is a “pronouncement of wisdom” by the central top management, which finally has the last word, but takes into account the findings from the bottom-up planning. This can be seen as a kind of democratic dictatorship.

In a nutshell: In bottom-up planning, the knowledge of the entire organization is integrated into the planning process. This ensures motivation for all employees, but can result in goals that are not very ambitious. In the top-down process, the problem is exactly the opposite: The goals are set ambitious, but the knowledge of the entire organization is not used and employees may be demotivated. The advantages of both procedures are combined in the countercurrent process.

3.5 Problems with Incentives through Planning

3.5.1 The Problem of Hidden Information

In the planning process, the connection between planning and remuneration leads to problems that, in the worst case, prevent the planning functions from being fully carried out. One reason lies in the way in which the

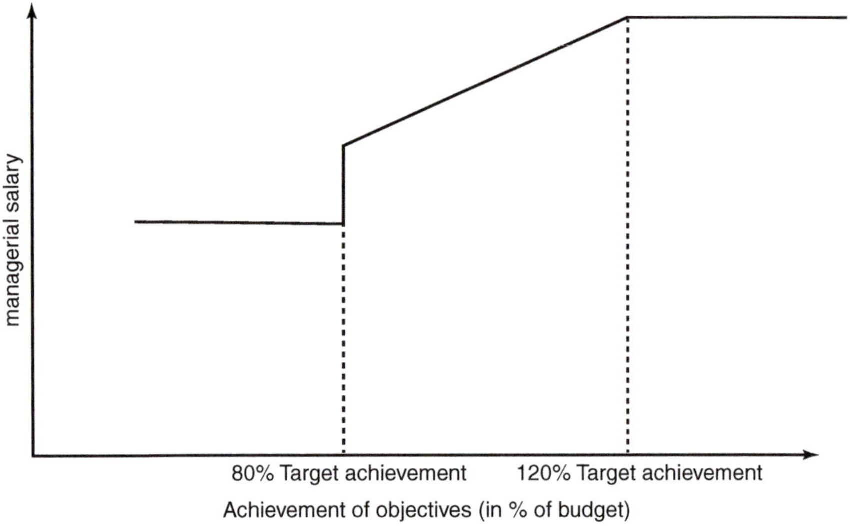

Fig. 3.5 Typical course of a variable remuneration

variable remuneration is determined (cf. Jensen 2003, pp. 386 ff.). Fig. 3.5 shows a typical variable remuneration agreement.

In addition to a fixed salary, the manager receives a variable share that is linked to the achievement of targets. Target achievement is represented as a percentage of the planned value. As a rule, a manager only receives a variable share at a certain target achievement level (in the example at 80% of the budget). If a car salesman has the target of selling 100 cars in a year, he receives a bonus of 0 for 70 cars. If the minimum target is not achieved, the manager gets nothing. At 80%, the manager receives a premium for having crossed the hurdle. The car salesman who would have gone empty-handed with 79 sold cars receives a premium of, for example, 2000 € for the 80th car because it represents the limit. From 80 cars, his variable salary increases linearly, the car salesman receives a bonus of, for example, 100 € for each additional car sold. However, the linear increase in remuneration is capped at 120% of target achievement, so that the car salesman receives no further bonus for the 121st car and beyond.

In such an incentive system, some possible distortions arise. The manager will do everything to reach the lower limit and realize the bonus for overcoming the hurdle. Even company-damaging behavior such as selling cars with too high discounts or sales manipulation can be used to always enjoy this bonus.

► Example: Damage caused by planning

Jensen (2003) reports on the Korean subsidiary of Lernout &Hauspie Speech Products NV. In order to achieve the set targets and thus create the conditions for their bonus, the management booked fictitious sales to a considerable extent. Between 1999 and 2000, 70% of the reported sales of 160 million US dollars were completely invented. ◄

If the car salesman should notice that he can no longer jump over the lower limit of 80%, his incentives change significantly. Now it is rational for the salesman to shift sales into the next period. This makes it easier to achieve the target next year. The bonus system ensures that it is irrelevant to the employee whether he achieves 50, 60 or 70% of the target, as there is no punishment system. The incentive to do nothing is further increased by the **"Ratchet Effect".** This was first described in socialist centrally planned economies (see Meyer and Vickers 1997). The planners take the current state as the starting point for the considerations for the next plan value. Once achieved, results cannot be undercut, but only exceeded. The English word "ratchet" describes a latch that can only be opened in one direction. For the car salesman this means that the shift of purchases into the next year not only makes it easier to achieve the target, but that the target accepted by the head office in the following year will be lower. It is clear that the activities of the car salesman do not contribute to the overall welfare of the company in such a situation: The potential car buyers are likely to go to the next car dealership instead of waiting any longer.

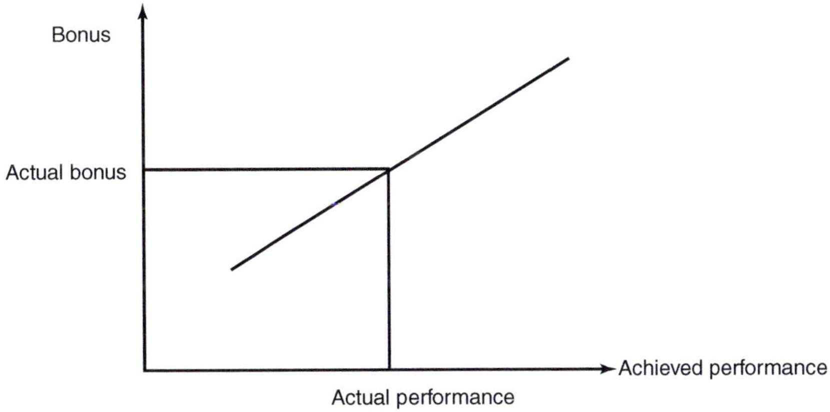

Fig. 3.6 Linear course of a variable compensation

If business is running exceptionally well and the car salesman reaches the upper bonus limit, all incentives for further efforts are lost again. Since the car salesman gets nothing from the 121st sold car, he will no longer make any effort to sell cars. Here too, the ratchet effect acts reinforcing.

Problems therefore always arise at threshold values. In the phase where a manager receives a linearly increasing bonus, these problems disappear. For this reason, Jensen (see Jensen 2003, p. 389) proposes a completely linear bonus calculation (see ◘ Fig. 3.6), so that the car salesman would receive the same amount of money for the first to the last sold car.

The problems shown in the planning can lead to considerable real economic consequences. Jensen (2003) describes the case of a manager of a beverage manufacturer who, in order to keep his goals low, deliberately underestimated the achievable sales figures. This resulted in insufficient production and the company had no products available during their most important sales period, the summer holidays. The planning could not fulfill its coordination function.

Furthermore, the communication function can also be disturbed, because honest communication does not take place. So the car salesman will not name the true sales volume that he expects for the coming year, but a lower one. However, the corporate headquarters is usually too far away to know the accurate information about future developments and is therefore dependent on the correct information of the company parts to receive a realistic plan.

3.5.2 The Weitzmann Schema

The problem of the conscious misleading of superiors in the planning process had, in addition to corporate practice, a special importance in the central administrative economies of socialism. The managers and employees of enterprises in the centrally planned economies received a bonus if they had achieved the plan set by the central planning office. In order to make this as easy as possible, the actual production possibilities were underestimated (Gutmann 1990). In response, incentive systems were created that included the honesty of the statements of the employees in the incentive calculation. In a discussion of various socialist incentive systems, Weitzmann (1976) (Ewert and Wagenhofer 2014, pp. 410 ff.) Described the following model, which is also often referred to as the **"Soviet incentive scheme"**.

The model is based on the assumption that the employee exactly knows the surplus x to be achieved in the future. The management, on the other hand, does not know this. The scheme differentiates between the actually achieved size x and the size x* reported by the management to the management. The bonus for the employees is linked to as much agreement as possible between x and x*. So the message of the truth is rewarded, while those who make false statements are punished. There must be a bonus factor a*, a_1, a_2 given with the condition $0 < a_1 < a^* < a_2$. The manager then receives the following bonus according to the Weitzmann scheme:

1. In the case that $x = x^*$: $a^* \cdot x^*$
2. In the case that $x > x^*$: $a^* \cdot x^* + a1 \cdot (x - x^*)$
3. In the case that $x < x^*$: $a^* \cdot x^* + a2 \cdot (x^* - x)$

When this system is applied, it pays off for decentralized managers to tell the truth.

▶ Example: Bonus calculation according to the Weitzmann scheme

Let's assume that a manager knows the value for the future profit of his sub-operation x = 200 exactly. The bonus factors are given with:

- $a1 = 0.1$
- $a^* = 0.2$
- $a2 = 0.3$

If he reports this truthfully, he receives as a bonus (Case 1):

$$x^* \cdot a^* = 200 \cdot 0{,}2 = 40$$

If he underestimates when submitting the plan and reports 100, he receives the following bonus (Case 2):

$$a^* \cdot x^* + a_1 \cdot \left(x - x^*\right) = 0{,}2 \cdot 100 + 0{,}1 \cdot (200 - 100) = 20 + 10 = 30$$

If he overestimates when submitting and reports 300, the manager receives the following bonus (Case 3):

$$a^* \cdot x^* + a_2 \cdot (x^* - x) = 0.2 \cdot 300 + 0.3 \cdot (100 - 200) = 60 - 30 = 30$$

It can be seen that the manager is rewarded by the Weitzmann scheme if he tells the truth. The maximum bonus is only given if the planned and the actual result match. ◀

The Weitzmann scheme leads to the fact that the one who tells the truth in the planning phase receives the highest bonus. The case that is rewarded in conventional budgeting processes, deliberately underestimating one's own performance and thus easily getting a bonus, is thwarted by the incentive scheme. However, it must be critically noted that the assumption of an exact knowledge of the actually achievable value is unrealistic. However, one can generally agree with the assumption that the one who enters the plan values knows better about the achievable values than the central controlling.

A variant of the Weitzmann scheme was practically applied in the DIY store chain OBI in the 1990s, which controlled its branches using the Weitzmann scheme (Creusen 1990).

3.6 Alternative Planning Approaches

Due to the problems in planning with hidden information, which endangers the functionality of the planning, many companies have become very skeptical or even completely dispense with budgeting. The Liechtenstein drill manufacturer HILTI has already abolished corporate planning worldwide in 2005.

Other companies continue to plan, but see the benefits of this instrument critically. According to an empirical study, controllers on average spend 120 days per year on creating the plan. Assuming approximately 220 working days per year (calendar year minus weekends and vacation or sick days), this represents more than half of the working year that a whole department is dealing with the creation of the plan (Nevries et al. 2009, p. 238). It is questionable whether this effort justifies the undisputed benefits of the plan.

From these considerations, various solutions arise. In particular, three solution approaches are represented in the theory and practice of controlling:

1. The **Better Budgeting** (improved planning/budgeting): Here, point-specific improvements are made to the traditional planning in order to address the largest points of criticism. Thus, corporate planning should focus on a few particularly relevant cost types and cost centers. The orientation towards the past should be given up as far as possible. Instead of the annual budget, the Better Budgeting uses a five-quarter view with a **Rolling Forecast**. This forecast makes a fine planning for the next quarter. The quarters 2 to 4 are taken over from the last Rolling Forecast planning. The fifth quarter is planned anew. Three months later, in turn, the nearest quarter is finely planned (the rough planning from the last

Rolling Forecast is refined and possibly changed accordingly). The quarters 2 to 4 are left unchanged or adjusted if necessary. Then a new fifth quarter is planned.

2. In the **Advanced Budgeting** instruments are used which should achieve a stronger market orientation and focus of the planning. Market orientation means that you should deal less with the company itself in the planning. This takes up the often expressed criticism that customer contact is neglected in the planning phase because the managers are busy with the company itself. With the focus, the criticism should be taken up that too many data are produced which are not used in the end. The method is strongly based on process cost accounting.
3. The **Beyond Budgeting** (overcoming planning/budgeting): Here, the traditional budgeting is thrown overboard as a whole and something entirely new is tried. This is the most revolutionary approach. Rigid concepts, as offered by traditional planning (target setting—target achievement with review after a fixed period of time) are no longer to take place. Instead, adaptive processes are to be established which take into account changes in the environment and can therefore be changed more quickly and which also maintain the performance of management over long periods of time. For example, one can imagine that the sales targets of a department can no longer be achieved due to a recession. This does not lead to a change of goals in the model of traditional budgeting.

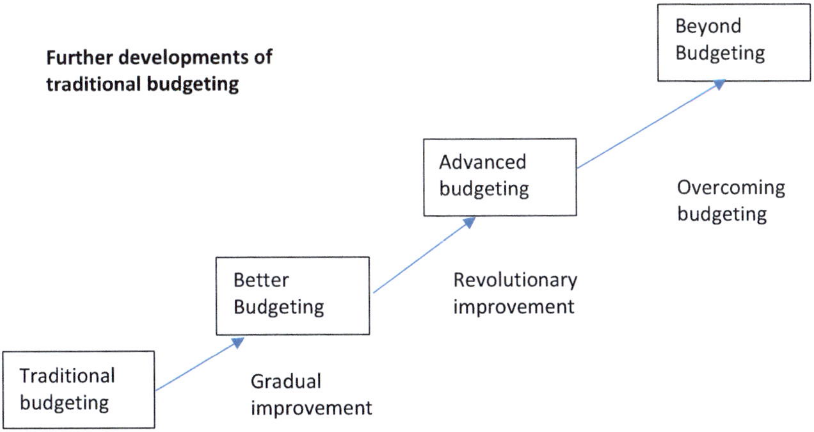

Fig. 3.7 Intensity of change of planning through alternative planning approaches. (Own representation based on Gleich et al. 2006, p. 25)

Instead, the manager already knows before the end of the planning period that he will not achieve his performance targets. Accordingly, he will be demotivated to approach his work for the next time. This leads to negative effects on the company alone through false incentive setting and planning mechanisms.

All methods have different requirements for the change of corporate planning: from gradual to revolutionary change to the overcoming of planning (see ◘ Fig. 3.7). Many companies adopt the methods for gradual improvement of planning or make use of individual elements from the concepts. The implementation of the very comprehensive concept of Beyond Budgeting is very rare, as it entails not only a cultural change but also considerable change costs. Companies from the Scandinavian area in particular, such as Volvo or Svenska Handelsbanken, have completely or partially dispensed with planning.

3.7 Learning Control

To the point

Planning deals with the future of the company. Through planning, all departments are brought to talk to each other about future actions, the activities of the individual departments are coordinated. In many cases, the fulfillment of the plan also leads to the distribution of a variable compensation. However, by linking variable compensation and planning, an incentive is created for employees not to tell the truth, but to set an easily achievable goal.

Many companies state the value orientation as a goal. The value from the perspective of the equity investors is the shareholder value. In order to determine this, the future expected free cash flows are discounted with the weighted capital costs (WACC), which represent the equity and debt capital costs according to the financing structure of the company. The WACC thus represents the hurdle rate that must be overcome in order to make an investment value-adding. If, in addition to the interests of the owners, the immediate wishes of the other stakeholders are also taken into account in the target setting, one speaks of stakeholder value. However, its clear quantification is problematic.

As a result of the manifold criticism of the traditional planning methodology, alternative planning approaches have been developed. These range from point-wise improvements (better budgeting) to a complete abandonment of planning (beyond budgeting).

Let's check

Consider whether the following statements are true or false:

- Planning is a means of getting the uncertainty in the company "under control".
- The controllers are responsible for the content of the plan.
- Planning management is the task of controlling.
- Planning has, among other things, the function of ensuring that departments talk to each other and coordinate with each other.
- Base targets are fundamental for the entire company and are above the operational targets.
- Operative and strategic goals are independent of each other because they involve different matters.
- Goals such as environmental protection and sustainability have become less important in the last decade according to empirical findings.
- Shareholder value refers to the value of the company from the perspective of the owners.
- WACC represents the minimum return of a company weighted by the cost of equity and debt.
- When the goals of other stakeholders are included in the goal setting of a company, it is called stakeholder value.
- Stakeholder value can be easily calculated using analytical methods.
- Goals should preferably be based on past results. This makes it very easy to identify potential for improvement.
- The ratchet effect states that a goal can never be set below the result achieved once for psychological reasons.
- Threshold values in bonus agreements can cause special problems.
- In the Weitzmann scheme (Soviet incentive scheme), the one who tells the truth in the planning is rewarded in the bonus calculation.

Connecting tasks

1. The medium-sized Internet company Maximal GmbH was founded by Mr. M. It has grown rapidly. Departmental structures are still lacking, as they are known from large companies. Mr. M. has hired you as a financial controller to support him. You will be given the task of designing a planning process. In doing so, you should make sure that the employees have to invest as little time as possible, but remain motivated. Furthermore, the planning process should take into account the dynamic development of the company in a rapidly changing environment. Make suggestions for the sequence of the planning.

2. In the last financial year, Minimal GmbH achieved sales in the North sales area of 1.2 MEUR. The management sets a target of 1.3 MEUR for the sales manager. In the planning meetings, the sales manager expresses his dissatisfaction, as this target level is unrealistic from his point of view. Last year, Minimal had an extraordinary order, the repetition of which is unrealistic. Assess this discussion situation! What compromise proposal would you make to solve the problem?
3. Vagabund Tours AG is a Swiss tour operator offering adventure tours in central Switzerland. In the future, the company wants to greatly expand its investment budget. The WACC should be the benchmark for the profitability of the investments. The owner of the company, Mr. Gutzeit, expects an interest rate of 16% on the capital he has invested. The company pays an average of 6% interest on the external capital. The company has a balance sheet total of 10 million CHF, of which 6 million CHF are equity and 4 million CHF are external capital. The applicable tax rate is 25%. Calculate the WACC!

Read and deepen

- Ehrmann H (2013) Unternehmensplanung. 6th ed. nwb, Herne.
  The book deals extensively with the process and the framework conditions of planning. It presents the basic questions divided into operational and strategic plans.
- Rapaport A (1994) Creating Shareholder Value. 2nd ed. Schäffer-Poeschel, Stuttgart.
  This book is relevant for all those who want to get an idea of the topic of shareholder value from first-hand sources. The original source is easy to read and still up-to-date despite the year of publication.

References

Albach H (1968) Betriebswirtschaftliche Anforderungen an eine langfristige Unternehmensplanung. ZfB 2/1968:3–19. (Ergänzungsband)
Ballwieser W (1995) Aktuelle Aspekte der Unternehmensbewertung. WPg 48:119–129
Behringer S (2012) Gewährleistungsrückstellungen nach HGB, IFRS und EStG. BBK 20/2012:945–950
Behringer S (2016) Verfahren der Unternehmensbewertung. In: Becker W, Ulrich P (ed) Praxishandbuch Controlling. Springer Gabler, Wiesbaden, pp 491–507
Behringer S (2018) Konzerncontrolling, 3. edn. Springer, Wiesbaden
Brühl R (2016) Controlling. Grundlagen einer erfolgsorientierten Unternehmenssteuerung, 4. edn. Vahlen, München

Cardinal LB, Miller CC, Kreutzer M, TenBrink T (2015) Strategic planning and firm performance. In: Mumford M, Frese M (Hrsg) The psychology of planning in organizations. Research and applications. Routledge, New York, pp 260–288
Clarkson MBE (1995) A stakeholder framework for analyzing and evaluating corporate social performance. Acad Manag Rev 20(1):92–117
Creusen U (1990) Controlling-Konzept der OBI-Gruppe. In: Mayer E, Weber J (eds) Handbuch Controlling. Schäffer-Poeschel, Stuttgart, pp 874–887
Cyert RM, March JG (1995) Eine verhaltenswissenschaftliche Theorie der Unternehmung. Schäffer-Poeschel, Stuttgart
Ewert R, Wagenhofer A (2014) Interne Unternehmensrechnung, 8. edn. Springer, Berlin
Gleich R, Greiner O, Hofmann S (2006) Better, Advanced und Beyond Budgeting: Von der Evolution zur Revoluntion. In: Gleich, Hoffmann, Leyk (Hrsg) Planungs- und Budgetierungsinstrumente. Haufe, Freiburg, pp 23–38
Gutenberg E (1983) Die Produktion, 24. edn. Grundlagen der Betriebswirtschaftslehre, Vol 1. Springer, Berlin
Gutmann G (1990) Volkswirtschaftslehre. Eine ordnungstheoretische Einführung. Kohlhammer, Stuttgart
Heinen E (1971) Grundlagen betriebswirtschaftlicher Entscheidungen. Das Zielsystem der Unternehmung, 2. edn. Gabler, Wiesbaden
Helbling C (1993) DCF-Methode und Kapitalkostensatz in der Unternehmensbewertung falls kein Fair Market Value. Schweizer Treuhänder 67:157–164
Horváth P, Dambrowski J, Jung H, Posselt S (1985) Die Budgetierung im Planungs- und Kontrollsystem der Unternehmung – Erste Ergebnisse einer empirischen Untersuchung. Betriebswirtschaft 1985(2):138–155
Jensen MC (2003) Paying people to lie: the truth about the budgeting process. Eur Financ Manag 9:379–406
Jung RH, Heinzen M, Quarg S (2016) Allgemeine Managementlehre, 6. edn. Erich Schmidt, Berlin
Klein R, Scholl A (2004) Planung und Entscheidung. Vahlen, München
Kosiol E (1967) Zur Problematik der Planung in der Unternehmung. Z Betriebswirtschaft 37:77–96
Krag J, Kasperzak R (2000) Grundzüge der Unternehmensbewertung. Vahlen, München
Krolak T, Rönnpag C, Stawinoga M, Gerl F (2011) Controlling in Familienunternehmen 2010 – Entwicklungen und Trends. In: Eckhard G (Hrsg) Schriftenreihe des Norddeutschen Instituts für Familienunternehmen, Vol 1. GHS, Göttingen
Küpper HU, Friedl G, Hofmann C, Hofmann Y, Pedell B (2013) Controlling. Konzeption, Aufgaben, Instrumente, 6. edn. Schäffer-Poeschel, Stuttgart
Locke EA, Latham GP (1984) Goal setting: a motivational technique that works! Prentice Hall, Upper Saddle River
Macharzina K, Wolf J (2017) Unternehmensführung, 10. edn. Springer, Wiesbaden
Meyer MA, Vickers J (1997) Performance comparisons and dynamic incentives. J Polit Econ 105:547–581
Miller CC, Cardinal LB (1994) Strategic planning and firm performance: a synthesis of more than two decades of research. Acad Manag J 37:1649–1665
Müller-Stewens G, Lechner C (2011) Strategisches Management. Wie strategische Initiativen zum Wandel führen, 4. edn. Schäffer-Poeschel, Stuttgart
Nagel M, Mieke P (2014) BWL Methoden: Handbuch für Studium und Praxis. utb, Konstanz

Nevries P, Strauß E, Goretzki L (2009) Zentrale Gestaltungsgrößen der operativen Planung. Z Control Manag 53:237–241
Schäffer U, Weber J (2015) Controlling-Trends & Benchmarks. WHU-Otto Beisheim School of Management, Vallendar
Schmalenbach E (1934) Selbstkostenrechnung und Preispolitik, 6. edn. Glöckler, Leipzig
Schreyögg G, Koch J (2010) Grundlagen des Managements, 2. edn. Springer, Wiesbaden
Steinmann H, Schreyögg G (2005) Management, 6. edn. Gabler, Wiesbaden
Stoffel K (1995) Controllership im internationalen Vergleich. Gabler, Wiesbaden
Sull DN (2005) Strategy as active waiting. Harv Bus Rev 83(9):120–132
Ulrich H, Probst GJB (1995) Anleitung zum ganzheitlichen Denken und Handeln: Ein Brevier für Führungskräfte, 4. edn. Haupt, Bern
Weber J, Schäffer U (2020) Einführung in das Controlling, 16. edn. Schäffer-Poeschel, Stuttgart
Weber J, Bender M, Eitelwein O, Nevries P (2009) Von Private Equity Controllern lernen. Wiley-VCH, Weinheim
Weitzmann ML (1976) The new soviet incentive model. Bell J Econ 7:251–257
Wild J (1974) Grundlagen der Unternehmensplanung. Rowohlt, Reinbek

The Control Function of Controlling

Contents

S. Behringer, *Financial Controlling*,
https://doi.org/10.1007/978-3-658-40527-4_4

4

Learning Agenda

The control function represents the synthesis of the two controlling functions described in ▶ Chap. 2 (information function) and ▶ Chap. 3 (steering function). The target (planning from the control function) and the actual situation (information from the information function) are compared and it is controlled how the two values differ. On the one hand, there is a purely mathematical activity: How do both differ? More demanding than this easily automatable activity is the question of what the differences are and what conclusions can be drawn from the deviations. In particular, the control function often requires the psychological intuition of controllers, as control is associated with negative feelings in those controlled.

The control function of controlling		
Basics of the control function	What is the purpose of control in companies? How does the process of control work in companies?	▶ Sect. 4.1
Actual-to-target comparison and deviation analysis	How do you determine quantity and price deviations? How do you determine and interpret the secondary deviation?	▶ Sect. 4.2
Control and result prediction	Why is result prediction important and what role does controlling play in this?	▶ Sect. 4.3
Problem areas of the control function	Where are psychological problems in the control function? How should one deal with sunk costs?	▶ Sect. 4.4

4.1 Basics of the Control Function

Control is often associated with negative connotations. Who wants to be controlled? Controls are rarely welcomed in organizations. They are usually seen as annoying, unwanted or even hated, they are unpopular (Gabele 1982, p. VII). Whoever controls wants to impose their opinion against resistance.

It has already been pointed out that controlling is often mistakenly reduced to control (▶ Chap. 1). However, control does indeed belong to the tasks of controlling, even if it is not the exclusive task.

Remember!

Control can be understood as a comparison between planned and actual values that have arisen from operational action (cf. Frese 1968, p. 53). Thus, control is nothing other than the other side of planning. Planning develops the target values for the company, control checks compliance with the planned values by comparing them with the actually achieved values.

The relationship between planning and control is therefore strong: "Planning without control is pointless, control without planning is impossible." (Wild 1982, p. 44).

Control follows a three-step process (Weber and Schäffer 2020, pp. 284 ff.):

1. A target-actual comparison is made. This comparison is a purely technical process that can also be automated. However, the accuracy of the data used must also be checked. It is important to ensure that a target-actual comparison can only work if the target data have been generated using exactly the same rules as the actual data.
2. In the second phase, the causes of the target-actual deviations are analysed. In doing so, controlling compares the planning assumptions with the actual conditions as reflected in accounting.
3. In the third phase, corrective measures are then derived to help close the gap between target and actual. In this third phase, the controller works together with the areas to be controlled. Controllers usually do not have the necessary specialist knowledge to be able to determine corrective measures on their own. Of course, this only happens if there are negative deviations from the plan. Positive deviations from the plan can also have their cause in wrong assumptions. This must also be addressed again in the next planning process.

Control thus serves essentially to influence behaviour. This also contributes to the fact that the person controlled experiences a learning effect. The deviation between target and actual is caused by an action or omission of the person controlled. The consequences are reflected in the target-actual deviation. Ultimately, control thus contributes to the better implementation of goals. Through control, the achievement of goals is always present and the responsible managers have to comment throughout the whole business year on how they want to achieve certain goals that seem to be out of sight. Studies have shown that human behaviour is influenced by control, the announcement of control or simply the presence of a control institution (cf. Churchill and Cooper 1966). So the mere announcement of controls can lead to employees increasing their efforts. Therefore, despite the negative connotations associated with it, control is extremely important for entrepreneurial action.

4.2 Actual-Plan Comparison and Deviation Analysis

The actual-plan comparison is usually automated in the monthly reports that the controlling department usually prepares for management on the first working days of a new month. These reports are intended for internal use and are intended to inform management about developments in relevant areas.

There are standard reports that are delivered to a fixed group of recipients at fixed times. For example, in large companies there is usually a monthly report for management. In addition, there are deviation reports that are then prepared by controlling when certain thresholds are exceeded or undershot. If, for example, there is a sales shortfall of 10% at a subsidiary, a deviation report is prepared. This widespread approach corresponds to management by exception, as the reports are only prepared exceptionally. In addition, there are individual reports that the controlling department prepares on request of a recipient and has specific content desired and defined by the addressee. With standard and deviation reports, the actual values are systematically compared with the planned values and a deviation is determined as a difference.

Often, deviations are made more vivid by graphical representations. There are traffic light displays that show in green that the area is above or at the planning level. With yellow there are deviations from the plan that endanger the achievement of the plan and red indicates that the plan is no longer achievable. It is also possible to represent this with speedometers, where the speedometer needle indicates whether you are in the red, yellow or green area. These graphics are automatically generated by the controlling software. This makes it easier for the manager to interpret the reports and he will quickly be made aware of where there is a need to question things more closely. This is usually necessary because managers have little time to deal intensively with the reports. For example, a study among Swedish managers showed that a manager has 9 min or less for 45% of his activities, for 42% of his activities he spends between 9 and 60 min and only in 13% of his activities does he have more than 60 min (see Tengblad 2006).

These short periods of time are not enough to analyze a concise monthly report in the required detail.

While the target-actual comparison is a mathematical task, the deviation analysis is a mixture of mathematical and intuitive tasks. The deviation analysis developed from cost accounting traces the deviations back to their mathematical causes. Costs are the product of quantity and price, so deviations can arise from three causes:

- **Quantity deviation:** A higher quantity was used than planned. Mathematically, the quantity deviation results as the product of the quantity change with the unit price.
- **Price deviation:** The prices for the production factors to be procured have changed compared to the plan. Mathematically, the price deviation results as the multiplication of price change and planned quantity.
- **Secondary deviation:** There is a part of the deviation that relates to both types of deviation at the same time and cannot be attributed to one or the other type theoretically. This is mathematically the product of price and quantity deviation.

In cost accounting, these three types of deviation are assigned to the responsibility of a cost center manager in total. But if you look at the individual elements, a different picture emerges: The price deviation cannot be held responsible, the quantity deviation can. The secondary deviation can also actually not be attributed to the responsibility of the cost center manager.

▶ Example: Price, quantity and secondary deviation at Kitty Fitness GmbH

Kitty Fitness GmbH manufactures weights, made of iron, among other things. The price for 1 kg of iron is planned at $p_p = 5$ €. The lowercase index p stands for the planned value. The cost center manager plans for a consumption quantity $x_p = 1000$. This results in the cost function for the plan K_p:

$$K_p = x_p \cdot p_p = 1000 \cdot 5 = 5000$$

After the planning period has ended, controlling creates a control statement. The lowercase i in the subscript index stands for actual values:

$$K_i = x_i \cdot p_i = 1100 \cdot 6 = 6600$$

Obviously, the cost center manager has missed the planned costs. 1100 kg of iron were consumed at a price of 6 €. The total deviation results in:

$$\Delta K = K_i - K_p = x_i \cdot p_i - x_p \cdot p_p = 6600 - 5000 = 1600$$

Since both price and quantity have risen above the planned value, both have contributed to the overall increase in costs. This can be calculated if, first of all, the planned and actual costs are inserted for the price, while only the planned costs remain for the quantity:

$$\Delta K_p = x_p \cdot p_i - x_p \cdot p_p = 1000 \cdot 6 - 1000 \cdot 5 = 6000 - 5000 = 1000$$

The price deviation is therefore 1000 €. If only the quantity is varied and the price is kept at the planned level, the quantity deviation can be calculated:

4

$$\Delta K_i = x_i \cdot p_p - x_p \cdot p_p = 1100 \cdot 5 - 1000 \cdot 5 = 5500 - 5000 = 500$$

Thus, the quantity deviation is 500 €.
The result is surprising. The total deviation is 1600 €, but the two types of deviation only explain 1500 € together. The question arises as to what the further increase in costs of 100 € is due to. The justification lies in the fact that the additional 100 kg of iron (i.e. the quantity deviation) also cost 1 € more per kg. But this effect is neither clearly a quantity nor a price deviation. It is therefore referred to as a **secondary deviation**. Mathematically, the secondary deviation results from the multiplication of the planned deviations of quantity and price, with the lowercase index s standing for the secondary deviation:

$$\Delta K_s = \left(p_i - p_p\right) \cdot \left(x_i - x_p\right) = (6 - 5) \cdot (1100 - 1000) = 1 \cdot 100 = 100$$

The secondary deviation therefore results from the interaction of price and quantity deviations. It is attributable to neither one nor the other. ◀

Even though the thoughts of deviation analysis were developed very strongly for companies with industrial production, the basic idea can also be transferred to companies in other industries. For example, an overrun of the personnel budget may be due to the use of more temporary workers or to an unplanned increase in wages and salaries. The additional use would be a quantity deviation, the salary increase a price deviation.

With this purely mathematical assignment, the factual reasons for the deviation have not yet been determined. The cause analysis can usually not be carried out by financial controlling alone. For this purpose, the support of the operational departments is required. For example, the use of temporary workers may have been caused by an increased sick leave or by higher requested services. Both have different recommendations for action: If the requested services are permanently higher, a more cost-effective permanent hiring may make sense. If, on the other hand, the short-term increased sick leave is responsible for the use of temporary workers, this has to be accepted and no further measures have to be taken. If the price deviation has arisen from an unexpectedly high tariff increase, the head of the department can not be held responsible for the exceeding of the personnel costs budget. If the cause lies in the fact that a departing employee is to be kept by an individual salary increase, the responsibility lies with the department head.

4.3 Control and Result Forecast

In addition to the pure control, controlling also takes over the function of forecasting the result of the company. The requirement for the accuracy of this forecast increases steadily in one business year - the closer the balance sheet date comes, the more precise the result must be predicted. However, the result forecast is also worth mentioning if significant deviations already occur early in the current business year. At the latest from the middle of the business year, it is considered to adjust the current objectives upwards or downwards if the objectives are no longer achievable or if it is already recognizable that the objectives will be achieved easily. From the middle of the business year, the new budgets are created, so that goals have to be found which take into account the current deviations from the plan.

Here, the work of financial controlling is again of external importance. Listed companies have to publish a profit warning if they do not reach their published profit forecast. The failure to then publish an ad-hoc announcement is classified as an offense. In Switzerland, the regulation is somewhat more generous: There it is only necessary to issue the profit warning if the deviation can lead to a significant loss in value, which is generally given as 10%. Both regulations show that despite the threat of fines, companies have a considerable margin of discretion.

In addition, controlling must assume its role as an entrepreneurial early warning system that recognizes risks and opportunities in good time. It plays a big role to recognize whether the observed deviations are short-term influences or long-term deviations, which can develop into existential crises. Here it is important that controllers quickly and intensively feedback their observations to the management.

The forecast also plays an important role in tax controlling. In addition to the targeted design of the tax balance sheet, the expected (i.e. budgeted) profits are the basis for the assessment of the advance tax payments set by the tax office. If there are greater deviations during the course of a financial year, it makes sense to report this to the tax office. As a rule, this will adjust the advance tax payment downwards. However, the tax authorities expect trusting data. This means that the reported change in results should not be changed again immediately, but should have reached a certain degree of stability.

In addition, forecasts of results receive special attention in special situations, e.g. in company valuation, which are required, for example, for an impending sale of the company. Caution is advised if company valuation is based solely on company planning. Pure company planning does not represent expectations, but rather aims to transport ambitious goals and motivate employees to work for the company (Behringer and Gleißner 2018).

4.4 Problem Areas of the Control Function

Just like all other functions of financial controlling, the image of the rational decision-maker or advisor is disturbed by cognitive distortions.

A widespread phenomenon is that complete re-evaluations of projects are not carried out in the event of negative deviations from the plan. If we consider a large-scale research project, for example for a new drug, it may happen that a project that was originally positive no longer pays off. The cause could be a delayed or too expensive achievement of milestones in the project. A rational decision-maker would have to completely re-evaluate this project and, based on the new findings, cancel it if the benefit of the cancellation is higher for the company than the continuation (cf. Meredith 1988, p. 31). Empirically, however, it can be seen that cancellation decisions are made too late (cf. Cheng et al. 2003, p. 64). The same phenomenon can be seen in all projects in which **sunk costs** arise. Sunk costs are costs that have already been incurred and are therefore irreversible. They are no longer decision-relevant because they cannot be changed anymore. However, managers do not like changes very much, and they find it difficult to really ignore costs that have already been incurred.

Reasons for this phenomenon can be found in the behavior of decision-makers. Psychologists and Nobel Prize winners in economics Kahnemann and Tversky (Kahnemann and Tversky 1979, pp. 263 ff.) have developed the **Prospect Theory** to explain the behavior of people under uncertainty. Basically, people are risk-averse in their decisions, but the behavior changes decisively when the current result is above or below a reference point. This is a key difference from the expectation utility theory, which is considered rational, after which decision-makers maximize the expected utility of a decision in each case (Beck 2014, p. 120). The reference point relevant to controlling in many cases is the plan value. If the decision-maker currently has a positive plan deviation, he decides risk-averse in order not to lose the already achieved (but not yet realized) profit. However, if there is a negative plan deviation, the decision-maker seeks the risk in order to use every chance to make up for the already incurred (but not yet realized) loss.

If this effect is supplemented by the findings of **mental accounting** (cf. Thaler 1985), the problem of what accounting faces in its function as a rationality advocate becomes even clearer. According to mental accounting, people assign certain expenses to categories, similar to the accounts of external and internal accounting. This means that a decision-maker keeps a mental account on which the sunk costs of the research project are recorded. This mental account then has to be closed when the project is abandoned, the loss is realized at that moment. If the project is continued, there is a chance that the project will make up for the current loss and thus the account can be balanced or even closed positively. That people have a tendency to keep loss-making mental accounts open for longer has been found in a whole series of experimental studies:

Example: mental accounting

The phenomenon can be illustrated by a thought experiment (cf. Thaler 1999, p. 191). Let's assume that a student has bought a pair of expensive shoes. In the shoe store they were comfortable and didn't press. But when they were first worn, they turned out to be uncomfortable. Thaler makes the following predictions about how to deal with this problem: First, the student will try to wear the shoes, the more expensive the shoes were, the more attempts she will make. At some point she will stop wearing the shoes. But she won't throw them away, she'll keep them. The more expensive the shoes were, the longer she will keep them. Ultimately, the student will throw the shoes away at some point, regardless of how expensive they were. Namely, when the purchase price is mentally written off. This behavior is likely to be familiar to most consumers.

It can be summarized that projects are often stopped too late, areas are closed too late or other decisions are postponed for too long. For controllers it is important to know these cognitive distortions. Since the financial controller is not the decision maker himself, he has the possibility to act more rationally here and to point out the end of a project at the right time in his role as advocatus diaboli. The fact that controllers have this important task also speaks in their favor that experimental studies have shown that managers are more likely to invest in loss-making businesses if they themselves have made the decision that led to the loss-making business (see Staw and Fox 1977).

Another psychological aspect that is of great importance in controlling is **framing.** This describes that the formulation of a decision problem can influence the choice of alternative. This is also a contradiction to the classical assumption of behavior of the rational decision maker. This would be completely unaffected by the formulation of a decision problem. Since financial controllers are the preparers of decisions, they have direct influence on the formulation of decision templates. The Prospect Theory is also relevant here, which describes the special loss aversion of people. If an action is described with losses or negative properties, it is avoided. If the logically equivalent alternative is formulated positively, the same decision makers would choose it. The classic example of such a decision alternative is the Asian Disease Problem (Tversky and Kahneman 1981). Two groups are fictitiously made health ministers of their countries and have to decide on treatment options. For the first group the alternatives are:

1. If therapy A is used, 200 people will be saved.
2. If therapy B is used, 600 people will be saved with a probability of one third. With a probability of two thirds, no one will be saved.

The first group, which was confronted with these two possible answers, chose the safe alternative A for the most part. However, with their expected benefits, the two are equivalent.

The second group was faced with the following alternatives:

1. With therapy C, 400 people die.
2. With therapy D, there is a one-third probability that no one will die. With a two-thirds probability, 600 people will die.

With this formulation, therapy D is chosen predominantly. However, all four therapies are actually the same. The alternatives that emphasize the loss (death of people) are less likely to be chosen. In addition to the Prospect Theory, an alternative explanation is given that the formulation acts as a heuristic - that is, it helps to solve complex and complex situations with simplifications. This effect was experimentally demonstrated in a study: One group of subjects was shown a glass of water filled to the 1-liter mark. They were briefly led out of the room and, upon their return, the glass was only half full. This group described the glass as predominantly half empty.

It was different with another group that first saw an empty glass and, after their return, described the half-filled glass as half full (McKenzie 2004). This idea can also be applied to the Asian Disease Problem. Alternatives 1 and 4 describe the situation completely, while alternatives 2 and 3 only provide an incomplete description of the situation. Depending on how the subjects supplement the given information on their own, this has an impact on their decision (Stocké 2000).

It is important for the controller to know these effects. In text information - for example, the commentary on the monthly report - he himself has to be careful how certain things are formulated. With inputs from other departments, for example comments on investment or project proposals, he must not fall for framing effects so that he fulfills the task of ensuring rationality of leadership.

As part of its tasks, controlling must subject the templates for management to a "debiasing". The English term "bias" refers to a distortion. Controlling must distort the information again so that management can make the decision undistorted in the short time available.

4.5 Learning Control

To the point

Control is not the only task of financial controlling, but it is an extremely important element of its activity. For every entrepreneurial action, control is significant, since only by announcing controls can the persons concerned change their behavior.

The control in controlling begins with a planned-actual comparison. Planned data are compared with actually achieved data. First, there is a mathematical consideration of the deviations. The causes are determined in the deviation analysis. There are deviations that are due to price deviations (a supplier has changed his prices) and those that are due to quantity deviations (more quantity was consumed). In addition, there is the secondary deviation, which results from the multiplication of changed quantity and changed price and is therefore not exactly classifiable.

In the analysis of which consequences should be drawn from deviations, psychological factors play an important role. In particular, distortions in connection with irreversible costs (sunk costs) lead to the fact that projects are not abandoned even though they are no longer profitable. Controlling must know these distortions as an advocate of rationality in the company and take them into account in its recommendations.

4

Let's check

Consider whether the following statements are true or false:

- Planning and control are closely related to each other.
- The control begins with the analytical search for deviation causes.
- The search for deviation causes can be easily automated.
- Because of the time pressure in management, it makes sense to visualize certain issues.
- Quantity and price deviations are the sole reasons for deviations from the plan.
- Secondary deviations arise from the product of quantity and price deviations.
- Sunk Costs are irreversible costs that should be ignored in a decision-making process.
- The Prospect Theory states that, among other things, gains are weighted more heavily by people than losses.
- Framing refers to the influence of the presentation of a decision problem on the chosen decision.

Connecting tasks

1. The following prices and quantities are planned for use in one cost center: The only material to be used is 120 kg. One kilo is to cost €14. In fact, 160 kg are used in the month. The price rises to €16 per kg. Calculate the price, quantity, and secondary deviation and consider the responsibility for each type of deviation.
2. A new airport is to be built in a large German city to accommodate the expected significant increase in the number of passengers. After five years of construction, it is apparent that the original plans were not feasible and that the project cannot be profitably continued in this form, as the necessary renovations would be significantly more expensive than the demolition of the existing sections and a complete new construction elsewhere. Discuss this scenario in the context of the sunk cost problem!

Read and deepen

- Kahnemann D (2012) Thinking fast and slow. Penguin London.
  Nobel laureate Daniel Kahneman has summarized his main findings on the psychological influences on human decision-making behavior in an easy-to-read popular science book. It is extremely helpful for every controller to know the distortions of human behavior presented here.

References

Beck H (2014) Behavioral economics. Springer, Wiesbaden
Behringer S, Gleißner W (2018) Die Unternehmensplanung als Grundlage für die Unternehmensbewertung. WPg 71(5):312–319
Cheng MM, Schulz AK, Luckett P, Booth PJ (2003) The effects of hurdle rates on the level of escalation of commitment in capital budgeting. Behav Res Account 15:63–85
Churchill NC, Cooper WW (1966) A field study of auditing as a mechanism for organizational control. In: Lawrence J (Hrsg) Operational research and the social sciences. Springer, London, S 109–127
Frese E (1968) Kontrolle und Unternehmensführung. Gabler, Wiesbaden
Gabele E (1982) Vom technischen „Soll-Ist Vergleich" zur „Aktiven Kontrolle" in Organisationen. In: Thieme HR (Hrsg) Verhaltensbeeinflussung durch Kontrolle – Wirkung von Kontrollmaßnahmen und Folgerungen für die Kontrollpraxis. Erich Schmidt, Berlin, S VII–XV
Kahnemann D, Tversky A (1979) Prospect theory: an analysis of decision under risk. Econometrica 47:263–291
McKenzie CM (2004) Framing effects in inference tasks – and why they are normatively defensible. Mem Cogn 32(6):874–885
Meredith J (1988) Project monitoring for early termination. Proj Manag J 29:31–38
Staw B, Fox F (1977) Escalation: the determinants to a chosen course of action. Hum Relat 30(5):431–450
Stocké V (2000) Framing und Rationalität: Die Bedeutung der Informationsdarstellung für das Entscheidungsverhalten. Oldenbourg, München
Tengblad S (2006) Is there a new managerial work? A comparison with Henry Mintzbergs classic study 30 years later. J Manag Stud 43(7):1437–1461
Thaler RH (1985) Mental accounting and consumer choice. Mark Sci 4(3):199–214
Thaler RH (1999) Mental accounting matters. J Behav Decis Mak 12(3):183–206
Tversky A, Kahneman D (1981) The framing of decisions and the psychology of choice. Science 211(4481):453–458
Weber J, Schäffer U (2020) Einführung in das Controlling, 16. Aufl. Schäffer-Poeschel, Stuttgart
Wild J (1982) Grundlagen der Unternehmensplanung, 4. Aufl. Rowohlt, Reinbek

Digitization and Controlling

Contents

S. Behringer, *Financial Controlling*,
https://doi.org/10.1007/978-3-658-40527-4_5

Learning Agenda

Digitalization has had a great influence on many social and economic contexts. Financial controlling cannot close itself off to this. However, it is first necessary to clarify what is meant by the terms digitalization and also the associated terms such as artificial intelligence or big data. We then go on to look at the consequences of digitalization for controlling in particular: What are the concrete effects on the processes in controlling? This in turn has consequences for controlling departments and the requirements placed on controllers and their role in the company. In addition, we examine whether different requirements for controlling and the instruments used by it arise from digital business models.

Digitalization and Controlling		
Terms	What do the terms digitalization and artificial intelligence mean?	▶ Sect. 5.1
Digitalization of Controlling	Which processes within Controlling can be digitalized? What does digitalization mean for Controlling?	▶ Sect. 5.2
Controlling of digitalization	What challenges does digitalization of business models pose for Controlling? How can the Business Model Canvas be used as a tool in Controlling?	▶ Sect. 5.3

5.1 Terms "digitalization" and "artificial intelligence"

Digitalization, viewed purely from a technical perspective, refers to the conversion of texts, sounds, or other signals into numerical values (in bits and bytes). This is a prerequisite for being able to store and further process these signals. However, this narrow, very technical definition does not capture the core of the deeper social and economic dimensions of digitalization: digitalization refers to the widespread distribution of information technology with all its economic, social, and political consequences, which represent both opportunities and risks (Petersen 2020, p. 13).

Digitalization creates opportunities to process large amounts of data. In addition, more and more data is being produced by products, customers, websites, etc. Preparing this data and deriving useful statements from it is a key task of controlling—one of its core tasks is to provide management with information. This is discussed under the term Big Data. Big Data does not only aim at the amount of data (Volume), but also at the essential difference of the data, which can come from different sources (texts, numbers, videos, etc.). Artificial intelligence (AI) methods can be used for processing. The definition of AI is highly controversial in the sciences. As a rule of thumb, it is said that these are systems that are able to solve problems independently (Carbonell et al. 1983). A distinction is made between strong AI, which tries to imitate human thinking and ultimately also wants to reproduce emotions in machines. So far there have been no results—this form is still mainly the subject of science fiction literature. This is different in the case of weak AI. Here, solutions are being developed for narrowly defined problem areas (Buxmann and Schmidt 2019, pp. 6 f.). This is already happening successfully and is also being applied to fields that are directly relevant to controlling. A key instrument of AI is machine learning. Through experience, the systems try to learn in order to be able to make predictions about what will happen in the future. These methods are now also being applied to more complex systems, such as the recruitment of employees (see Dahm and Dregger 2019).

The special abilities that machines can develop through training are particularly evident in the application to the Asian board game "Go". DeepMind, a Google subsidiary, has developed a computer program called Alpha Go that can beat the best players in the world at Go. Go is considered one of the most complex games in the world—more complex than chess. The program was trained using played games between humans and thus developed into a superior opponent (Silver et al. 2016).

A large part of the theory and practice of controlling has been concerned in recent years with making these technologies usable for financial controlling. Controllers have two tasks in the context of digital transformation: On the one hand, they have to accompany their company as a business partner in digital transformation. They are the controllers of digitalization. On the other hand, they have to face digitalization themselves. Many areas of controlling are directly linked to digitalization: their own role, their own daily work has to be digitally transformed (Keimer and Egle 2020, p. 2).

5.2 Digitalization of Controlling

A core task of financial controlling is the provision of information. This task is very much shaped by digitalization and Industry 4.0. Industry 4.0 refers to the networking of machines, plants, products, etc. This makes data-based business models possible and significantly more data is available.

For example, sold machines that are already with the customer report back to the manufacturer how they are used and whether maintenance is necessary or not (Roth 2016, pp. 5 ff.). This is both a curse and a blessing: There is more information that can provide explanations for observed developments. At the same time, however, the risk of "information overload" also increases, i.e. the management as the recipients of the information being overwhelmed. It is all the more important to have a **gatekeeper** who monitors the quality, relevance and usefulness of the available information.

However, controlling will no longer be able to continue in the known form. Traditional controlling is at least partially called into question (Schäffer and Brückner 2019). The trend is coming from the Anglo-Saxon world to set up their own departments with data analysts or scientists. The goal of data analytics/science is to bring hidden knowledge to light from large and unstructured data sets using analytical methods. The data scientist starts his analysis without a specific hypothesis. He looks for hidden patterns in large unstructured data sets. The data scientist's task therefore begins with structuring large data sets and organizing them for analysis (cf. Davenport and Patil 2012). This trend leads to a potential competition for controllers. Some of the tasks of controlling can be well taken over by data scientists. However, there is often a lack of knowledge here on how to interpret numbers economically. On the other hand, controllers often lack the knowledge to evaluate the data sets.

The tool of **predictive analytics** will become increasingly important for corporate planning. Predictive analytics tries to recognize patterns by analyzing past data, possibly with the help of external data sets, and thus to predict future developments. This approach, which belongs to AI, also requires expertise in computer science, which is not available in traditional controller training.

Other data can also be evaluated here, not just pure financial information. For example, texts can be collected from social media channels and searched for certain word combinations that give an indication of how the reputation of a company or brand is developing (so-called sentiment analysis). This means that an important value driver can be directly taken into account in controlling data for many industries (Langmann 2019, p. 13).

Financial controllers must take into account that the automatically generated predictions implicitly influence the planning. So far, the forecasts have been created by controlling, now they are partly generated by machines. The planning results are predetermined by the algorithms used. The advantages of such a development are obvious: more reliable prognostic statements can be made in a shorter time. But the risk is just as evident. If planning assumptions are derived purely mechanically, they may lack the necessary reference to actual business. Controlling must recognize the pitfalls of the algorithms and transfer findings from old analyses into changed algorithms. First controlling software uses artificial neural networks, one of the methods of predictive analytics, to derive forecasts (e. g. Unit 4 Prevero, see Friedl 2019, p. 37), so that the entry into everyday life for controllers has already taken place.

However, an uncritical use of data analytics methods can lead to wrong decisions. The long-standing experience of controlling as a rationality assurance function of management must not be lost, just because there are supposedly better automated methods. These methods also need a qualitative input to be meaningful. Controllers are predestined to provide this input. But they have to assume the role and make their way to learn data analytics.

In addition, many processes in the finance department can be automated by robot process automation (RPA). Software can carry out business processes entirely or partially independently. In the financial sector, for example, this includes the booking of invoices, the checking of travel and expense receipts and the posting of payments (Langmann and Turi 2020). However, this releases personnel resources in the finance sector.

As a result of the digitalization of service provision or automated processes in sales (use of internet shops, etc.), significantly more data is generated that can potentially be used to support decision-making. In the course of digitalization, it can be assumed that these unstructured data will also automatically become structured information that management can use to support decision-making—the methods of information processing discussed under the keyword Big Data will support this. Controlling needs fewer employees to fulfill its tasks, which can save personnel in financial controlling. Overall, the digitalization in controlling and in the financial sector as a whole requires a significant restructuring. For the future profile of controllers, the need arises to acquire more and more computer-based knowledge.

Through easy-to-use software, the creation of reports is increasingly being shifted to the specialist departments. However, the integrity of the reports must still be ensured by controlling. Controlling is still to be the **"single source of truth"** that ensures that the reports are correct and complete. The management of the company continues to trust the reports verified by the controller. In addition, the controller will be increasingly involved in areas such as ad-hoc analysis or interpretation of reports.

The role of controlling as the exclusive provider of information is losing importance at all levels. At the same time, the requirements for the interpretation of the information provided are increasing, which also increases the requirements for controllers. But here too, automation brings about a relief in terms of craftsmanship. For example, the (technical) integration of external and internal accounting eliminates reconciliation between the different accounting circles. The interpretation of an integrated financial statement will gain more and more importance, but the very time-consuming analysis and explanation of differences in recognition and valuation will be eliminated. Controlling will therefore have to justify its added value for business support and its personnel strength differently in the future.

In a nutshell: Digitalization offers considerable opportunities for controlling. There are more options for controlling and preparing information. However, this also comes with a significant structural change: Manual tasks can be automated by AI and RPA. Controllers need good economic knowledge in addition to IT skills in order to be able to fulfill their role as business partners in the future.

5.3 Controlling of Digitalization

The digital world is often characterized by the abbreviation VUCA, which stands for volatility, uncertainty, complexity and ambiguity. The term was originally coined by the US armed forces to describe the multilateral world of the 1990s. Nevertheless, it has gained importance in describing the digital world. There is no doubt that market complexity has increased for most companies. Competition is now global, the pace of product development is higher, transparency for customers is much greater, resulting in almost exclusively buyer's markets. Controlling must also react to these developments, not only in its own processes, but also through adapted processes and instruments to adequately map digital business processes (Becker et al. 2016).

The task of controlling is not to assess the technical possibilities of digital innovations, but rather to assess their economic potential. Pampel (2018) distinguishes three areas of responsibility in which the financial controller must become active in digital business models:

1. **Innovation**: This is about assessing the novelty of a business model. This can be based on a completely new development or enable efficiency gains (e.g. through Industry 4.0 applications). But it is also conceivable that models enable closer customer loyalty, e.g. by integrating into social media. New possibilities for cooperation are provided by the collection

of data, e.g. from manufacturers for machines in connection with maintenance intervals.

2. **Scaling**: The task of the controllers in this phase is to check the prospects for success of the innovative business model. At this point it is about checking whether there are customers who are willing to pay something for the innovation and whether this price is sufficient to cover the costs and, in addition, to generate a reasonable profit. In this respect, the key figures used do not differ too much from the key figures traditionally used in companies. It is about sales, costs and other key performance indicators that have to be fulfilled by digital business models sooner or later.
3. **Strategic problems**: Companies have only limited resources available. At the beginning of a business model innovation, the resources for the digital innovation have to be made available. In the growth phase, it must be seen how the resources for the new business can be built up. In the third phase, a change of resources may then take place. It is no longer the analogue business model that the company carries. On the contrary: Resources must be withdrawn from the old business model and applied to the digital business model.

▣ Figure 5.1 illustrates the process. It can be seen that controlling is often entrusted with tasks that also play a role in analogue processes. Neu sind die Methoden zu Beginn der Implementierung von Geschäftsprozessen. Eine wichtige Rolle spielt dabei das **Business Model Canvas** (Osterwalder und Pigneur 2011). Dabei wird ein Geschäftsmodell in neun eng miteinander verknüpfte Komponenten geteilt, die einzeln betrachtet werden:

1. Value proposition: The innovation's value proposition for customers. What customer problem is being solved?
2. Key Resources: What resources are needed to implement the business model? Are they special technologies or skills? What financial resources are needed for implementation?
3. Key Activities: What activities does the company need to implement the business model and especially the value proposition? These can be, for example, certain marketing activities such as building a brand.
4. Key Partnerships: This describes which partners are needed in a business network to implement the business model. For example, do you need partners in technology development or a distribution partner?
5. Cost Structure: Based on the Key Resources, Activities and Partnerships that are necessary to fulfil the Value Proposition, a cost structure results, which is presented in this block.

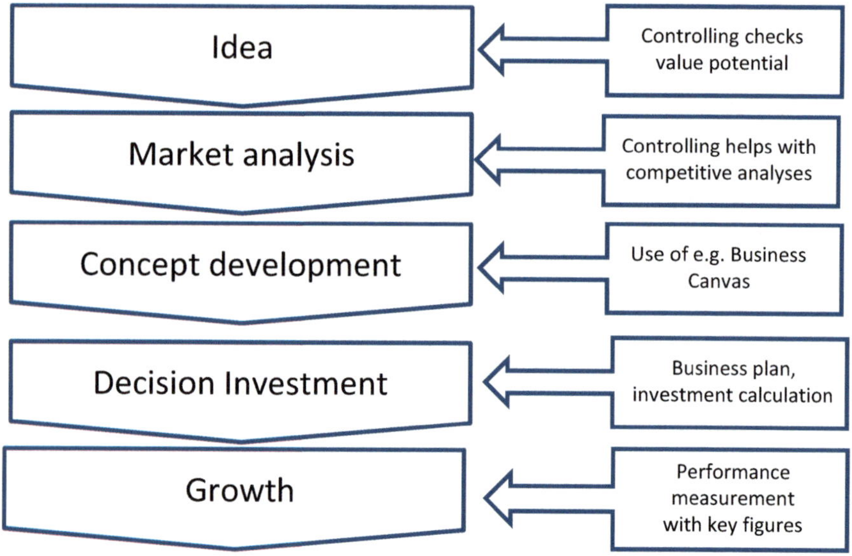

Fig. 5.1 Process of introducing digital business models (left) and tasks of financial controlling (right). (Source: Own creation based on Pampel (2018), p. 27)

6. Customer Segments: Here certain customer groups are described for which the Value Proposition could be interesting. The customer groups can be considered separately according to priority, e.g. in order of expected profitability.
7. Customer Relationship: This section contains the acquisition of customers and the care of customers. It is also about the type of relationship that one wants to have with one's customers. Do you want a long-term trusting relationship or do you rely on new customer relationships (walk-in traffic)?
8. Channels: This segment describes the communication channels to customers or customer groups. One question is, for example, whether the product is only sold online or also uses stationary sales channels.
9. Revenue Stream: Here is the key question of the business model, namely how customers pay and whether they are willing to pay for the value proposition.

With the Business Model Canvas, you get a good overview of the most important fields in the early stages of idea development that you need to make a decision whether or not to implement a business model. The most important areas for assessing a business model are represented on a canvas, so that they provide a good basis for decision-making. For the controller, it is a valuable tool in the examination of the corresponding business models.

5.4 Learning Control

To the point

Digitalization essentially means transforming information into bits and bytes for further processing using electronic methods. However, digitalization also entails far-reaching changes for financial controlling. In this context, certain technologies can be specifically helpful for controlling. These are primarily artificial intelligence (in its weak form), in which machines independently learn to solve narrowly defined problem areas. This can, for example, take the form of predictive analytics in the budgeting and forecasting of framework data. In addition, routine tasks can be automated through robot process automation. Additionally, controlling is changed in that digitalization decentralizes access to and creation of reports. Managers create their reports themselves. This eliminates a lot of manual work. However, the interpretation of reports becomes increasingly important for controllers, and management will continue to rely on the data quality of reports validated by controllers in the future.

Controlling digitalization is also a challenge for controlling. However, in the end, it all comes down to the same thing: Every business model must lead to an increase in value for the company. However, tools like the business model canvas can help to check the business idea and its feasibility.

Let's check

Consider whether the following statements are true or false:

- In many companies, the position of a data scientist has been created to deal with the search for patterns in large data sets.
- Artificial intelligence tries to better support decision-making by imitating human intelligence.
- The possibilities of digitalization increase the requirements on the controller to ensure data quality and good interpretations.
- Robot Process Automation automates many routine processes.

- Digital business models have fundamentally different success criteria than traditional business models. Profits are not so important.
- The Business Model Canvas represents the most important elements of a new business model in its components and connections.

Networking tasks

1. Think about how you can represent the following business model with the Business Model Canvas: You develop an app that shows how full buses and trains of public transport are in a large city. You assume that potential passengers are willing to pay for this information in order to be able to get on empty vehicles. You want to bring the advantages and the concrete implementability of your business model closer to a potential investor. Use the nine components of the Business Model Canvas to show the advantages!

Read and deepen

- Keimer I, Egle U (2020) Die Digitalisierung der Controlling-Funktion. Springer, Wiesbaden.
  The volume brings together contributions from theory and practice. In addition to the theoretical foundations, the book shows the application in companies through contributions from practitioners or interviews with controllers.
- Osterwalder A, Pigneur Y (2011) Business Model Generation: A Handbook for Visionaries, Game Changers and Challengers. Campus, Frankfurt.
  The original source for the Business Model Canvas is highly recommended. The book (in landscape format) gives visually clear hints for the application of the model.

References

Becker W, Ulrich P, Botzkowski T, Eurich S (2016) Controlling von Digitalisierungsprozessen – Veränderungstendenzen und empirische Erfahrungswerte aus dem Mittelstand. In: Obermaier (ed) Industrie 4.0 als unternehmerische Gestaltungsaufgabe. Springer Fachmedien Wiesbaden, Wiesbaden, pp 97–117

Buxmann P, Schmidt H (2019) Grundlagen der Künstlichen Intelligenz und des Maschinellen Lernens. In: Buxmann P, Schmidt H (Hrsg) Künstliche Intelligenz. Springer, Wiesbaden, pp 3–19

Carbonell JG et al (1983) An overview of machine learning. In: Michalski RS, Carbonell JG, Mitchell TM (Hrsg) Machine learning: an artifcial intelligence approach. TIOGA Publishing Co, Palo Alto, pp 3–23

Dahm M, Dregger A (2019) Der Einsatz von künstlicher Intelligenz im HR: Die Wirkung und Förderung der Akzeptanz von KI-basierten Recruiting-Tools bei potenziellen Nutzern. In: Arbeitswelten der Zukunft. Springer, Wiesbaden, pp 249–271

Davenport TH, Patil DJ (2012) Data scientist: the sexiest job of the 21st century. HBR, October

Friedl G (2019) Künstliche Intelligenz im Controlling. Controlling 31(5):35–38

Keimer I, Egle U (2020) Digital Controlling – Grundlagen für den erfolgreichen digitalen Wandel im Controlling. In: Keimer I, Egle U (ed) Die Digitalisierung der Controlling-Funktion. Springer, Wiesbaden, pp 1–16

Langmann C (2019) Digitalisierung im Controlling. Springer Gabler, Wiesbaden

Langmann C, Turi D (2020) Robotic Process Automation (RPA) - Digitalisierung und Automatisierung von Prozessen. Springer Gabler, Wiesbaden

Osterwalder A, Pigneur Y (2011) Business Model Generation. Campus, Frankfurt/New York

Pampel JR (2018) Digitale Horizonterweiterung - Begleitung der Innovation von Geschäftsmodellen durch das Controlling. Controlling 30(5):20–29

Petersen T (2020) Diginomics verstehen. Ökonomie im Licht der Digitalisieurng. utb, München

Roth A (2016) Einführung und Umsetzung von Industrie 4.0. Grundlagen, Vorgehensmodell und Use Cases aus der Praxis. Springer, Heidelberg

Schäffer U, Brückner u L (2019) Rollenspezifische Kompetenzprofile für das Controlling der Zukunft. Control Manag Rev 63(7):14–31

Silver D, Huang A, Maddison CJ, Guez A, Sifre L, van den Driessche G et al (2016) Mastering the game of go with deep neural networks and tree search. Nature 529:484–489

Trends in Controlling

Contents

S. Behringer, *Financial Controlling*,
https://doi.org/10.1007/978-3-658-40527-4_6

6

Learning Agenda

In the previous book, the knowledge you expect from textbooks has been presented. Chap. 6 deals with trends that are foreseeable but not yet fully developed. Therefore, the following sections should give you an insight into the expected developments and outline what challenges are likely to arise for controlling departments and controllers in the next few years. There are two development lines in particular that need to be considered: On the one hand, the pressure from the public but also the increased regulation is leading to sustainability becoming increasingly important. On the other hand, the legislator has significantly increased the obligations of companies, in particular listed companies, in terms of control, corporate governance and compliance. This has an impact on both the activity and the organization of controlling.

Trends in Controlling		
Controlling and Sustainability	What tasks arise from sustainability aspects for controllers? Why is it important that sustainability and controlling are integrated?	► Sect. 6.1
Controlling and risk management	What tasks are part of risk management? How can these be taken into account organizationally in financial controlling?	► Sect. 6.2
Controlling and compliance	What is the Business Judgement Rule and how does it affect controlling? What are the organizational relationships between compliance and controlling?	► Sect. 6.3

6.1 Controlling and Sustainability

The principle of sustainability goes back to classical forestry. Thus, the Freiberg forester Hans Carl von Carlowitz demanded in his work "Sylvicultura oeconomica" from the year 1732 that in one year no more wood may be felled than grows back (Dillerup and Stoi 2016, p. 78). The principle has been operationalized by the World Commission on Environment and Development set up by the United Nations under the chairmanship of the former Norwegian Prime Minister Gro Harlem Brundtland, who defined sustainable development in her 1987 report as meeting the needs of today's generation without jeopardizing the possibilities of future generations or restricting their needs (cf. WCED 1987, p. 25). This definition places the human being and his claims at the center. The natural environment remains a means to an end that can also be used by humans for the satisfaction of their needs.

When it comes to sustainability, it is not a fashion topic, as the "Fridays for Future" movements worldwide have shown. It will remain and increasingly influence business decisions. Not only the legislator ensures greater transparency in the field of sustainability with ever new regulations. In the meantime, it is also investors, employees, customers and the public directly interested in the company that directly and without compromise demand sustainable behavior. Various initiatives by non-governmental organizations and in international organizations have long been putting pressure on companies to report on their impact on society and the environment. Transparency will inevitably increase. Greenwashing, as many corporations have done or are still doing, will become increasingly difficult in the future due to legal requirements. The ecological and social consequences of decisions must actually be taken into account. Otherwise, stakeholders can sanction the company in many ways. This development inevitably requires that controlling also deals with these issues. If it does not, other departments will move into this gap and play an increasingly important role in decision-making. With the CSR Implementation Act passed by the German Bundestag in 2017, many companies are now required to publish non-financial indicators in the areas of environment and social affairs. The obligation to publish also creates pressure on management to integrate social and green aspects into their decision-making calculations. The institution that acts as a rationality assurance of leadership must therefore also open up to the non-financial sphere of companies. This requires different instruments for data collection, different knowledge in the analysis and thus overall different competencies for controllers.

Financial controlling must integrate aspects of sustainable corporate governance at the process level. This also changes the role that controllers play. If the concept is actually taken seriously, it is inevitably necessary to seriously consider sustainable aspects in decision-making preparation, which will also be reflected in changed requirements for the competence of controlling.

For controllers, it will become more important to position themselves as a sustainable department. There is often the prejudice that controlling and sustainability do not go together (Colsman 2016). However, if sustainability is a serious corporate goal, it must also be controlled—that is, it must become part of normal corporate controlling. Therefore, it is very important for both areas that controlling and sustainability flow from one source—only then is it guaranteed that sustainability aspects are also really taken into account in top management decisions. Otherwise, a division threatens—here the corporate controlling, there the sustainability. Neither goal will be served.

6.2 Controlling and Risk Management

6

The German Stock Corporation Act (AktG) was supplemented by paragraph 2 by the Act on the Control and Transparency of Companies (KontraG). This reads:

"The Board of Directors shall take appropriate measures, in particular to establish a monitoring system, in order to identify developments endangering the existence of the company at an early stage."

This results in the obligation of a company to establish an **internal control system** and an early detection system at least for risks endangering existence. A risk management system is not necessarily associated with this. The legislative justification assumed that risky business can have an impact on the assets, financial and earnings situation of a company and that, by means of the measures required by the law, they can be recognized. However, according to prevailing opinion, a risk management system is not necessarily required. If the boards of directors of stock corporations ignore these duties, this will be interpreted as a breach of their duty of care. In the event of damage, this will result in claims for damages.

In the **German Corporate Governance Code**, which started as a voluntary self-commitment but has now acquired a legally relevant status through the declaration of compliance according to § 161AktG, the duty of the management board to ensure appropriate risk control and risk management is codified. The obligations of the companies are additionally reinforced by the provision of §§ 289 Abs. 5 and 315 Abs. 2 No. 5 HGB, which states that capital companies must describe in the annual report the essential features of their internal risk management system with regard to accounting. There are also some legal obligations to maintain a special risk management system at international level.

Controlling plays a special role in this area. The connection to the rationality assurance function is obvious: By implementing the legal requirements, the risks are identified at an early stage, which creates information that the management needs to control the business. This also makes a contribution to the assurance of rationality. For these reasons, it makes sense not to set up too many parallel structures in a company, but to look for synergies with existing departments. This can be done, for example, by integrating the activity into controlling. The extensive discussion in the literature on the identity of risk management and risk controlling is not pursued here (cf., for example, Kajüter 2008). The essential tasks of risk controlling are (Vanini 2012, pp. 23 f.):
- To generate information about potential risks and make it available to the relevant decision-makers;
- To coordinate and interlock the risk management process with other processes in controlling, for example the planning process;
- To develop methods and make them available to the relevant management levels in order to identify and assess risks;
- To support the management in the performance of the tasks of risk assessment and risk management.

In summary, it can be said that risk control takes over part of the statutory obligations of corporate management to manage risks. However, without taking over these part tasks, the effective implementation of the remaining risk management tasks remains difficult. Since some legal and factual requirements have arisen in recent times that companies have to meet in the field of governance, risk and compliance. The problem is that this often leads to parallel structures, since all obligations are to be mapped by a separate department. This can be avoided by a targeted search for synergies. Controlling offers itself as a department for the integration of risk management, as there are many synergies in terms of content. In addition, both theoretically and organizationally, a close connection between the activities can be seen.

For corporate management, in particular the members of the board of directors of stock corporations, the obligation and the associated liability risks have increased considerably. Since these are personal risks of management, in practice, these issues often form the focus of activities.

6.3 Controlling and Compliance

Controllers can make a significant contribution to successful compliance management (cf. Hirsch and Fiack 2015, pp. 69 ff.), just as compliance managers can make a significant contribution to effective controlling. Compliance refers to all measures taken by a company to comply with legal and other externally imposed rules as well as internal rules.

As part of their information provision, controllers should also provide compliance management with targeted information. **Opportunistic behavior** of employees to prevent, is the task of controlling in the context of their rationality assurance function. Where opportunism turns into rule-breaking behavior, it becomes the task of compliance management. This particularly affects the incentive systems, which are conceptually and operatively controlled to a large extent by controlling.

The waves of regulation of recent years, which have been triggered by corporate scandals, the financial crisis and a general skepticism of the general public towards the management of large companies, will have an increasingly strong influence on controlling. Controllers are predestined to take on a decisive, often also the responsible role for the legally impeccable decision-making preparation. The reporting system also receives an increasingly important role for the legal protection of the executive board and the supervisory board. Controlling has a key function in protecting against liability.

The distinction between breach of duty and business decision will also gain in importance. The business decision is regulated by law through **the Business Judgement Rule**. This is codified in § 93 para. 1 sentence 2 AktG for the stock corporation, whereby one can assume that it also has an impact on GmbHs. There are also similar rules in Austria and Switzerland. Accordingly, a breach of duty by a management board member is not always the case if, in a business decision, a management board member was allowed to reasonably assume that he had decided in the interests of the company on an appropriate basis of information.

An important criterion for management board members to be able to rely on the Business Judgement Rule is the "appropriate information base". The Federal Constitutional Court has brought the Business Judgement Rule to the following concise form: A management board member is not legally liable for the success of a decision, but for a carefully taken decision. This is where the core area of the activity of controlling is affected. It is the responsibility of controlling to provide the information in an appropriate breadth and depth. When preparing documents for decision-making, controlling must increasingly take into account that they may become evidence in a trial.

However, the increased responsibility is also rewarded: The legislator assumes an as objective rationality as possible in his guiding principle of appropriate decision-making. This makes the rationality-securing function of controlling increasingly important. Controlling should use its core competence here and in particular intensify the cooperation with compliance departments.

Due to the numerous overlaps between controlling and compliance, one can consistently think to the end that the two departments are merged (Behringer 2017). Where compliance is integrated into existing departments, legal departments are usually merged with compliance, and internal audit is sometimes merged with compliance in the personnel department. Controlling is rarely mentioned in theoretical and empirical work. However, a look at the biographies of many compliance officers shows that they often have a past in controlling. This is probably due to the fact that both staff functions have a broad view of the company, have to deal with legal norms and at the same time need a broad understanding of business administration.

Nevertheless, one will notice an incompatibility of the summary of controlling and compliance. The reason for this is the clearly different task description of the two departments. They both have different roles vis-à-vis the management, in which they should both but immediately cooperate. The controller's task is to secure economic rationality. He is a consultant to management in terms of the company's objectives and target achievement. The role is that of an active consultant in the strategic and operational area, demanding rationality. The compliance manager, on the other hand, has the task of ensuring compliance with external and internal regulations. In terms of business operations, he has rather a passive role, with a veto right in business transactions that do more harm than good. In this respect, there will be a double structure mentioned above (► Sect. 6.2).

6.4 Learning Control

To the point

Regulation creates new fields of activity and challenges for controllers. The legislator is giving companies more and more tasks. One of them is risk management. Here, an integration into controlling should be sought wherever possible. This does not necessarily apply to compliance management due to the different tasks. However, close cooperation between controlling and compliance is always advisable. The Business Judgement Rule intervenes in the core area of financial controlling, requiring a precise documentation of decision-making bases in order to distinguish between decisions that trigger liability (because they are based on insufficient information) and those that do not trigger liability. With the CSR Implementation Act, which was passed by the German Bundestag in 2017, there is also the need to publish non-financial data for companies. This puts pressure on companies to actually take social and sustainable aspects into account in entrepreneurial decision-making. This should be an incentive for controllers to also deal with these issues in the future. Sustainability must be controlled on the one hand, on the other hand, only by an integration is it actually ensured that sustainability aspects are also taken into account in decisions at top management level.

Let's check

Consider whether the following statements are true or false:

- Sustainability refers to the ability of resources to be available for future generations.
- The adoption of the CSR Implementation Act has resulted in many large companies having to publish non-financial data.
- Stock corporations must have a system in place to identify risks that threaten their existence.
- Stock corporations must have a risk management system in place.
- The Business Judgement Rule leads to entrepreneurial decisions not resulting in liability.
- Compliance and controlling should always be conducted in one department.

Connecting tasks

1. Kitty Fitness GmbH is a medium-sized provider of fitness equipment that is offered both by traveling salespeople and by its own online shop. The production of the equipment is outsourced to external production companies, mainly in China. The Controlling department currently consists of two controllers who create an annual plan and carry out a monthly reporting system for the management. In addition, Controlling is available to the two managing directors for ad-hoc analyses and projects from finance and accounting. Consider the effects on the organization and activities of Controlling of Kitty Fitness GmbH through the trends

a. Sustainability
b. Risk management and
c. Compliance
can arise.

Read and deepen

- Vanini U (2012) Risikomanagement. Schäffer-Poeschel, Stuttgart. This book gives a good insight into risk management and risk control. It is designed as a basic textbook.
- Behringer S (2018) Compliance kompakt, 4th ed. Erich Schmidt Verlag, Berlin. This editor's volume offers a comprehensive insight into the theory and practice of compliance management in a compact form. The various facets of compliance management are presented in a condensed form.

References

Behringer S (2017) Rationalität trifft Rechtskonformität. Zur Zusammenarbeit von Controlling und Compliance. Control Mag 42(2):4–9
Colsman B (2016) Nachhaltigkeitscontrolling. Springer Gabler, Wiesbaden
Dillerup R, Stoi R (2016) Unternehmensführung, 5. Aufl. Vahlen, München
Hirsch B, Fiack S (2015) Compliance-Management und Controlling. ZRFC 10(2):68–73
Kajüter P (2008) Rolle der Internen Revision im Risikomanagement-System. In: Freidank CC, Peemöller VH (ed) Corporate Governance und Interne Revision. Handbuch für die Neuausrichtung des Internal Auditings. Erich Schmidt Verlag, Berlin, pp 109–126
Vanini U (2012) Risikomanagement. Grundlagen, Instrumente, Unternehmenspraxis. Schäffer-Poeschel, Stuttgart
WCED World Council of Economic Development (1987) Our common future. Oxford University Press, Oxford

Supplementary Information

S. Behringer, *Financial Controlling*, https://doi.org/10.1007/978-3-658-40527-4

Tips for Studying and Learning

The section "Tips for studying and learning" was written by Andrea Hüttmann.

Study!

Studying requires a different kind of learning than you are used to from school. Studying means diving into a subject, dealing intensively with matters, penetrating things deeply. Studying also means taking initiative, working independently, setting goals autonomously instead of waiting for specific work assignments. Successfully completing a degree requires the ability to develop effective behavior appropriate to the phase of life and the institution—this includes, among other things, functional learning and examination strategies, successful time management, a healthy portion of courage and a lot of proactive will to shape. Below you will find some tried and true tips that will give you orientation when studying, a graphical overview of which is shown in ◘ Fig. A.1.

Read a Lot and Quickly

Studying, as described above, means diving into a subject. We can do this best by simply reading a lot at first. From the learning method—reading, underlining, writing out—which we usually practice in school, we have to say goodbye in our studies. It takes too long and robs us of valuable time that we should rather invest in reading. Of course it makes sense to take notes here and there or to discuss things with others. But writing out our own texts systematically is not a recommended method in our studies—at least not across the board. Reading more and more quickly …

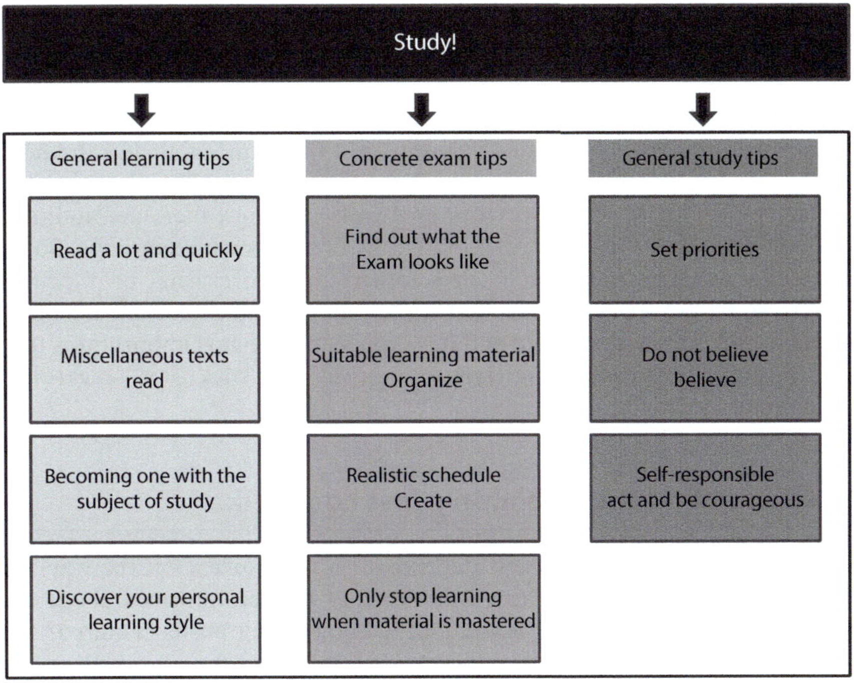

Fig. A.1 Tips at a glance

Become One with Your Field of Study

Beyond all pragmatism, we as students of a subject should be deeply interested in this subject as a whole. A burning interest does not necessarily have to exist from the beginning, but should be ignited during the course of a study. But please do not wait in a passive position to be inspired, but make sure that your field of study concerns you. As a rule, enthusiasm arises when we combine the contents to be studied with everyday topics: If we read newspapers and specialist magazines, for example, we understand which role the contents studied by us play in current events and which trends they are subject to; if we do internships, we experience that we can contribute valuable things with our know-how—often already after a few semesters. Last but not least: Things are usually fun when we master them. Before mastering comes engagement: So engage yourself and become one with your field of study!

Discover Your Personal Learning Style

Beyond some generally valid learning recommendations, every student has to find out for himself when, where and how he can learn most effectively. There are the larks who can concentrate best in the morning and the owls who move their learning phases into the evening and night. There are the visual learners who prefer to write and look at things; there are auditory learners who use, for example, audiobooks or their own recordings. Some prefer index cards of different sizes, others make overviews on flipchart sheets, some can learn by heart best while walking, others do this in a hammock. It doesn't matter where and how you learn. What is important is that you find an effective learning style for yourself and stick to it—regardless of comments from third parties.

Find out What the Upcoming Test Looks Like

The way you prepare for a test depends to a large extent on the way the upcoming test looks. Therefore, it is essential to keep informed about the type of test. Is rote learning asked for? Is knowledge transfer required? Do you have to present facts independently? Is a look over the edge of the plate required? Ask your lecturers. They don't have to answer you, but most lecturers are pleased with smart questions that attest to the interest of the students and will give you some hints in some form. Ask students in higher semesters. There is always a way to find out things. Whether you do it and how depends on the extent of your courage and your pro-activity.

Stock up on Suitable Learning Materials

If you know what kind of test is coming up, you have already won a lot. Now you need learning materials to work with. Never use the notes of others—they are unreliable in terms of content and not created from your head. Choose materials you can rely on and to which you have access. As a rule, a mixture is recommended—for a normal semester final exam, for example, your lecture notes, one or two relevant books on the subject (preferably one by the lecturer who sets the exam), a reference work (often available online today), possibly exam-preparatory books, for example from the textbook collection of your university library.

Create a Realistic Schedule

A realistic schedule is an integral part of a solid exam preparation. Approach the topic pragmatically and answer the following questions: How many weeks do I have until the exam? On how many days per week do I (realistically) have how much time to prepare for this exam? (At this point you are shocked and disappointed at the same time, because always not nearly as much time is available as you think you need.) If you know how many hours you have available for preparation, determine when you will work on which material. Now enter your plans in your schedule and see how you cope. If a schedule turns out to be unrealistic, change it. But never work without a schedule!

End Your Learning Phase Only When the Material is Mastered

A learning phase is only over when the material you wanted to cover in this unit is also covered. Most students are too lenient with themselves here and only orient themselves by time. The time window you have reserved for a certain amount of material is only one parameter of your plan. The other parameter is the material. And a learning unit is only over when you have achieved what you wanted to achieve. Be very disciplined and strict with yourself here. If you know that you are not allowed to get up when the time is up, but only when the work is done, you will work more concentrated and faster.

Set Priorities

You have to set priorities in your studies, because you cannot invest the same enormous amount of time in all subjects. Professors and lecturers have the habit of regarding the subjects they teach as the most important of all. Accordingly, every teacher will approach you with an unattainable expectation of your accompanying studies. Stay here completely sober and ask yourself the following questions: Which exams do I have to pass this semester? In which ones are good grades really important to me? Which subjects interest me the most or are the most important for the overall context of my studies? Last but not least: Where do I get the most credits? Depending on how you answer these questions, your commitment to exam preparation will vary. Decisions of this kind are not malicious demonstrations of disinterest in studies, but simply a matter of survival.

Don't Believe any Rumors

There are hardly any places where more rumors are spread than at universities—students love to increase dropout rates that they have heard by 10–15%, turn stories from oral exams into horror stories, and twist information from the examination office. Don't believe any of this and get all the important information from where you are qualified and reliable answers are given. 95% of the stories told at universities are simply invented and the result of "Chinese whispers".

Act Responsibly and be Brave

Self-responsibility and courage are basic attitudes that pay off more than in studies. As students, you have much more freedom than as pupils: You do not always have to be present, nobody is disappointed in you personally if you do not pass a test, no one holds a moral sermon if you have not done your homework, it is nobody's job to make sure you get along. So whether you are successful in your studies or not is of no concern to anyone but yourself. Consequently, only one university will be successfully left, which manages to act responsibly on its own conviction. The ability to self-management is therefore the soft skill from which university graduates benefit most in their later lives. At the same time, universities are institutions that instill a sense of respect in many students: professors are not necessarily seen as confidential contacts, the amount of material does not seem to be mastered, the institution with its many offices, committees and examination regulations is not transparent. But whoever is intimidated will be the loser. It is about developing courage, forging one's own way, proceeding with healthy self-confidence and also taking a pro-active approach in exams. Countless people have gone this way before you. You will make it too!

Andrea Hüttmann is a professor at the accadis University of Bad Homburg, head of the "Communication Skills" department and an expert in the training of students' soft skills. As a coach, she is also active on the free market and accompanies companies, private individuals and students in change projects and development wishes (▶ www.andrea-huettmann.de).

Glossary

Accounting External accounting which is addressed to external addressees and is prescribed by law.

Actual Costs Costs actually incurred.

Additional Costs Costs that are not included in the expenses (external accounting) and additionally find their way into internal accounting.

Administrative Department Frequent organizational classification of controlling, administrative departments have only indirect management functions. They advise, analyze and prepare decisions. Adminstrative departments such as controlling often have a high informal power.

Balanced Scorecard Balanced system of indicators that consists of a financial perspective, a customer perspective, an employee perspective and a process perspective. All indicators used should have a reference to the vision and mission of the company. The individual indicators should be interrelated in cause-and-effect relationships.

Benchmarking Systematic comparison between different companies with regard to business relations.

Beta Factor The beta factor measures the relative systematic risk of a security. One of the central figures of the Capital Asset Pricing Model.

Bottom-up Planning The planning variables are created by the employees and only compiled and accepted by the management.

Bounded Rationality Limited rationality that every human has. It consists of limitations of knowledge, limitations of anticipation of consequences of action and the limitations of known options.

Business Judgement Rule Regulated in §93 para. 1 sentence 2AktG: A breach of duty by a managing director of a stock corporation is not given if he was allowed to assume that he decided in the interests of the company on an appropriate level of information.

Capital Asset Pricing Model (CAPM) Model of capital market theory, in which prices for risky assets are to be determined analytically in equilibrium.

Cash Cash and book money balances in the company. They are needed to maintain liquidity.

Cashflow Balance of receipts and payments of a company, i.e. the change in liquid assets.

Contribution Margin Difference between the revenues of a product and its variable costs.

Costs and Revenues Measures of internal accounting. Costs are valued consumption of resources oriented to objectives. Revenues are the results of the business process of creating value.

Cost Center Accounting Stage of cost and revenue accounting in which costs are grouped according to their place of occurrence (department, etc.).

Cost Unit Accounting Stage of cost and revenue accounting in which costs are charged to outputs. Costs can be charged to individual products (cost object piece accounting) or to time units (cost object time accounting).

Cost of Goods Sold Accounting Stage of cost and revenue accounting in which costs are grouped according to their subject matter.

Countercurrent Process Synthesis of top-down and bottom-up planning. In practice the most widespread.

Effective A measure is effective if the resources used are suitable to achieve the set goal.

Efficient A measure is suitable if the resources used are in a reasonable relationship to the goal.

Equity Part of the total capital of a company. That part which has been left to the company by the owners.

Expenditures and Revenues Quantities of external accounting. Affect the equity of a company (expenditures—negative; revenues—positive).

Fixed Costs Costs which are independent of the actual employment of an enterprise.

Formal Objectives Financial objectives of a company.

Free Cashflow Cash which has been generated within the company and which is available for distribution to equity holders after all profitable investments have been made.

Debt Part of the total capital. That part which was left to the company by external enterprise.

Goals Desirable future states. Starting point of the planning.

Index Figures Key figures in which absolute figures of different periods are set in relation to each other.

Individual Costs Costs which can be directly attributed to a cost bearer.

Information Overload Management's inability to cope with too much information.

Kaizen Continuous improvement of business processes.

Law of Compensation of Planning The minimum sector (usually the sales of a product) is the reference point of planning. All processes are oriented towards it.

Line Function Departments with disciplinary authority.

Liquidity Ability of a company to meet its payment obligations on time (dispositive liquidity) or the money-nearness of assets (structural liquidity).

Management Approach IFRS guideline. The procedure in internal and external accounting should be the same. External investors should be able to assess decisions with the same information as management.

Material Goal The material goal of a company determines the goods and services to be sold.

Means-end Rationality Leading concept of controlling, the measures are effective and efficient.

Mission Part of strategic management, in which the purpose of the company is laid down.

Normal Costs Costs that arise when an operation is normally utilized (with normal material consumption).

Operational Accounting Internal accounting that is supposed to help support management decisions. The company is free in its design.

Opportunity Costs Costs of the opportunity missed.

Other Costs Costs that have a factual correspondence in expenses but are shown in different amounts.

Overhead Costs Costs which are not attributable to a cost center.

Partial Costing Instruments of cost and performance accounting, which only work with variable costs. They are suitable for making better decisions in the short term.

Planned Costs Normal costs that are extended by analytical considerations. They are planned for future periods.

Planning Prospective thinking that is supposed to anticipate future action. The core task of controlling is planning management. Only things that can be influenced are planned.

Planning Target Function Achieving the plan values is a prerequisite for achieving a variable compensation.

Predictive Analytics By analyzing past data, attempts are made to recognize patterns that can be concluded from future developments.

Price Deviation Deviation between planned and actual costs due to higher prices for input factors.

Process Sequence of activities. Can be output-induced, i.e. they are variable from the employment of a cost center or output-neutral, i.e. they are independent of the employment of a cost center.

Process Cost Accounting Method of cost management, which is intended to achieve better allocation of overheads in particular.

Production Costs Costs which are used to value the stocks in the balance sheet. The calculation of the production costs must comply with the legal basis.

Quantity Deviation Deviation between planned and actual costs due to higher consumption.

Ratchet Effect Observed effect in planning: plan figures are formed from the past and the past value is increased, a reduction is not possible, as it would have a demotivating effect.

Relational Numbers Indicators in which connections are made between different sizes.

Return on Investment Key figure of the DuPont analysis. States how much has been earned with the invested capital.

Secondary Deviation Deviation between planned and actual costs, which is due to both price and quantity deviations.

Shareholder Value Company value from the perspective of shareholders. Corresponds to the enterprise value, i.e. the share price of a share multiplied by the number of shares.

SMART-Method Instrument of the Goal Setting Theory. According to this, goals should be specific, measurable, challenging, realistic and timely.

Stakehoder Claim groups on a company.

Sunk Costs Sunk costs, i.e. costs that cannot be changed and are therefore not decision-relevant.

Target Costing Method of cost management, which starts from the achievable market price and derives the maximum permissible costs from this.

Top-down Planning The planning dimensions are set by the management without the involvement of the employees.

Variable Costs Costs that depend on the actual employment of an enterprise.

Variance Analysis The aim of this task of controlling is to identify causes of deviations between actual and planned values.

Vision Vision is part of strategic management. In it, the long-term objectives of the company are laid down.

WACC Weighted capital costs that are used to discount cash flows in investment accounting and company valuation. (Weighted Average Cost of Capital).

Working Capital A key figure for measuring liquidity. Difference between current assets (circulating assets) and current liabilities.

References

Albach H (1968) Betriebswirtschaftliche Anforderungen an eine langfristige Unternehmensplanung. ZfB 2/1968:3–19. (Ergänzungsband)

Bach N (2006) Analysis of the empirical Balanced Scorecard research in the German-speaking area. Control Manag 50:298–304

Baetge J (1998) Bilanzanalyse. IDW-Verlag, Düsseldorf

Ballwieser W (1995) Aktuelle Aspekte der Unternehmensbewertung. WPg 48:119–129

Barth T (2016) Planning in connection with the IFRS balance sheet and valuation. In: Becker W, Ulrich P (eds) Handbook of Controlling. Springer, Wiesbaden, pp 529–549

Beck H (2014) Behavioral economics. Springer, Wiesbaden

Becker W, Ulrich P, Botzkowski T (2016a) Controlling in the Mittelstand. In: Becker W, Ulrich P (eds) Handbook of Controlling. Springer, Wiesbaden, pp 583–603

Becker W, Ulrich P, Botzkowski T, Eurich S (2016b) Controlling of digitalization processes—change trends and empirical experience values from the Mittelstand. In: Obermaier (ed) Industry 4.0 as an entrepreneurial design task. Springer Fachmedien Wiesbaden, Wiesbaden, pp 97–117

Behringer S (2012) Warranty provisions according to HGB, IFRS and EStG. BBK 20/2012:945–950

Behringer S (2016) Verfahren der Unternehmensbewertung. In: Becker W, Ulrich P (eds) Praxishandbuch Controlling. Springer Gabler, Wiesbaden, pp 491–507

Behringer S (2017) Rationalität trifft Rechtskonformität. Zur Zusammenarbeit von Controlling und Compliance. Control Mag 42(2):4–9

Behringer S (2018) Konzerncontrolling, 3rd edn. Springer, Wiesbaden

Behringer S, Gleißner W (2018) Enterprise planning as the basis for enterprise valuation. WPg 71(5):312–319

Blase S, Müller S, Reinke J (2012) Progress in the harmonization of internal and external accounting through the management approach of IFRS. KOR 12(10):352–359

Britzelmaier B (2013) Controlling: Basics, Practice, Fields of Action. Pearson, Munich

Brühl R (2015) Wie Wissenschaft Wissen schafft. UVK, Konstanz

Brühl R (2016) Controlling. Grundlagen einer erfolgsorientierten Unternehmenssteuerung, 4th edn. Vahlen, München

Buxmann P, Schmidt H (2019) Grundlagen der Künstlichen Intelligenz und des Maschinellen Lernens. In: Buxmann P, Schmidt H (eds) Künstliche Intelligenz. Springer, Wiesbaden, pp 3–19

Carbonell JG et al (1983) An overview of machine learning. In: Michalski RS, Carbonell JG, Mitchell TM (eds) Machine learning: an artifcial intelligence approach. TIOGA Publishing Co, Palo Alto, pp 3–23

Cardinal LB, Miller CC, Kreutzer M, TenBrink T (2015) Strategic planning and firm performance. In: Mumford M, Frese M (eds) The psychology of planning in organizations. Research and applications. Routledge, New York, pp 260–288

Cheng MM, Schulz AK, Luckett P, Booth PJ (2003) The effects of hurdle rates on the level of escalation of commitment in capital budgeting. Behav Res Account 15:63–85

Churchill NC, Cooper WW (1966) A field study of auditing as a mechanism for organizational control. In: Lawrence J (ed) Operational research and the social sciences. Springer, London, pp 109–127

Clarkson MBE (1995) A stakeholder framework for analyzing and evaluating corporate social performance. Acad Manag Rev 20(1):92–117

Colsman B (2016) Sustainability Controlling. Springer Gabler, Wiesbaden

Creusen U (1990) Controlling Concept of the OBI Group. In: Mayer E, Weber J (eds) Handbook Controlling. Schäffer-Poeschel, Stuttgart, pp 874–887

Cyert RM, March JG (1995) A behavioral theory of the firm. Schäffer-Poeschel, Stuttgart
Dahm M, Dregger A (2019) The use of artificial intelligence in HR: The effect and promotion of the acceptance of AI-based recruiting tools by potential users. In: Work worlds of the future. Springer, Wiesbaden, pp 249–271
Davenport TH, Patil DJ (2012) Data scientist: the sexiest job of the 21st century. HBR, October 90(10):70–76
Dechene C (2016) Financial statement ratios and financial statement analysis. WISU 44:469–476
Deimel K, Heupel T, Wiltiner K (2013) Controlling. Vahlen, Munich
Dellmann K (2002) Key figures and key figure systems. In: Küpper HU, Wagenhofer A (eds) Dictionary of accounting and controlling, 4th edn. Schäffer-Poeschel, Stuttgart, pp 940–950
Dierkes S, Kloock J (2002) Kostenzurechnung. In: Küpper HU, Wagenhofer A (eds) Handwörterbuch Unternehmensrechnung und Controlling, 4th edn. Schäffer-Poeschel, Stuttgart, pp 1177–1186
Dillerup R, Stoi R (2016) Management, 5th edn. Vahlen, Munich
Eisenführ F (1966) Requirements for the information content of commercial annual financial statements. Diss., Kiel
Epstein MJ, Wisner PS (2001) Using a balanced scorecard to implement sustainability. Environ Qual Manag:1–10. ▶ https://doi.org/10.1002/tqem.1300
Ewert R, Wagenhofer A (2014) Internal corporate accounting, 8th edn. Springer, Berlin
Feil P, Yook K-H, Kim I-W (2004) Japanese target costing: a historical perspective. Int J Strateg Cost Manag 5:10–19
Frese E (1968) Kontrolle und Unternehmensführung. Gabler, Wiesbaden
Friedl G (2019) Künstliche Intelligenz im Controlling. Controlling 31(5):35–38
Gabele E (1982) From the technical "should-is comparison" to "active control" in organizations. In: Thieme HR (ed) Behavioral influence through control—effect of control measures and consequences for control practice. Erich Schmidt, Berlin, pp VII–XV
Gleich R (2011) Performance Measurement: Concepts, Case Studies and Basic Scheme for Practice, 2nd edn. Vahlen, Munich
Gleich R, Greiner O, Hofmann S (2006) Better, Advanced und Beyond Budgeting: Von der Evolution zur Revoluntion. In: Gleich R, Hoffmann S, Leyk S (eds) Planungs- und Budgetierungsinstrumente. Haufe, Freiburg, pp 23–38
Gutenberg E (1983) Die Produktion, 24th edn. Grundlagen der Betriebswirtschaftslehre, vol 1. Springer, Berlin
Gutmann G (1990) Volkswirtschaftslehre. Eine ordnungstheoretische Einführung. Kohlhammer, Stuttgart
Hauschildt J (1971) Entwicklungslinien der Bilanzanalyse. Z Betriebswirtsch Forsch 33:335–351
Heinen E (1971) Grundlagen betriebswirtschaftlicher Entscheidungen. Das Zielsystem der Unternehmung, 2nd edn. Gabler, Wiesbaden
Helbling C (1993) DCF-Methode und Kapitalkostensatz in der Unternehmensbewertung falls kein Fair Market Value. Schweizer Treuhänder 67:157–164
Hirsch B, Fiack S (2015) Compliance-Management und Controlling. ZRFC 10(2):68–73
Hitz JM, Jenniges V (2008) Publizität von Pro-forma-Ergebnisgrößen am deutschen Kapitalmarkt. Z Intern Kapitalmarktorientierte Rechn 2008(4):236–245
Hopper TM (1980) Role conflicts of management accountants and their position within organization structures. Acc Organ Soc 5:401–411
Horváth & Partner (2011) Performance management im Einkauf 2011: den Wertbeitrag des Einkaufs aktiv steuern und optimieren. Horvath & Partner, Stuttgart

Horváth P (2002) Controlling. In: Gaugler E, Köhler R (eds) Entwicklung der Betriebswirtschaftslehre. 100 Jahre Fachdisziplin. Schäffer-Poeschel, Stuttgart, pp 340–360
Horvath P, Lamla J (1996) Kaizen Costing. krp 40:225–240
Horvath P, Tani T (1997) Japanese-German comparison of target cost management. Working paper
Horváth P, Dambrowski J, Jung H, Posselt S (1985) Die Budgetierung im Planungs- und Kontrollsystem der Unternehmung – Erste Ergebnisse einer empirischen Untersuchung. Betriebswirtschaft 1985(2):138–155
Horvath P, Kieninger M, Mayer R, Schminak C (1993) Prozeßkostenrechnung – oder wie die Praxis die Theorie überholt. DBW 53:609–628
Horvath P, Gleich R, Seiter M (2020) Controlling, 14th edn. Vahlen, München
ICV (2013) Leitbild – Internationaler Controller Verein 2013. ▶ https://www.icv-controlling.com/de/verein/leitbild.html. Accessed 03 März 2017
Jensen MC (2003) Paying people to lie: the truth about the budgeting process. Eur Financ Manag 9:379–406
Jung RH, Heinzen M, Quarg S (2016) Allgemeine Managementlehre, 6th edn. Erich Schmidt, Berlin
Kahnemann D, Tversky A (1979) Prospect theory: an analysis of decision under risk. Econometrica 47:263–291
Kajüter P (2008) Rolle der Internen Revision im Risikomanagement-System. In: Freidank CC, Peemöller VH (eds) Corporate Governance und Interne Revision. Handbuch für die Neuausrichtung des Internal Auditings. Erich Schmidt Verlag, Berlin, pp 109–126
Kaplan RS, Norton DP (1996) Translating strategy into action: the balanced scorecard. Harvard Business School Press, Boston
Kaplan RS, Norton DP (2001) Transforming the balanced scorecard from performance measurement to strategic management. Account Horiz 15:147–160
Keimer I, Egle U (2020) Digital Controlling – Grundlagen für den erfolgreichen digitalen Wandel im Controlling. In: Keimer I, Egle U (eds) Die Digitalisierung der Controlling-Funktion. Springer, Wiesbaden, pp 1–16
Klein R, Scholl A (2004) Planung und Entscheidung. Vahlen, München
Kosiol E (1967) Zur Problematik der Planung in der Unternehmung. Z Betriebswirtschaft 37:77–96
Krag J, Kasperzak R (2000) Grundzüge der Unternehmensbewertung. Vahlen, München
Krolak T, Rönnpag C, Stawinoga M, Gerl F (2011) Controlling in Familienunternehmen 2010 – Entwicklungen und Trends. In: Eckhard G (ed) Schriftenreihe des Norddeutschen Instituts für Familienunternehmen, vol 1. GHS, Göttingen
Küpper HU, Friedl G, Hofmann C, Hofmann Y, Pedell B (2013) Controlling. Konzeption, Aufgaben, Instrumente, 6th edn. Schäffer-Poeschel, Stuttgart
Lambert C, Sponem S (2012) Roles, authority and involvement of the management accounting function. A multiple case-study perspective. Eur Account Rev 21:565–589
Langmann C (2019) Digitalisierung im Controlling. Springer Gabler, Wiesbaden
Langmann C, Turi D (2020) Robotic Process Automation (RPA) – Digitalisierung und Automatisierung von Prozessen. Springer Gabler, Wiesbaden
Laux H (1995) Erfolgssteuerung und Organisation. Springer, Heidelberg
Littkemann J, Michalik C (2004) Instrumente des operativen Beteiligungscontrollings. In: Littkemann J, Zündorf H (eds) Beteiligungscontrolling. Neue Wirtschafts-Briefe, Herne, pp 146–167
Locke EA, Latham GP (1984) Goal setting: a motivational technique that works! Prentice Hall, Upper Saddle River
Macharzina K, Wolf J (2017) Unternehmensführung, 10th edn. Springer, Wiesbaden
Maiga AS, Jacobs FA (2008) Extent of ABC use and its consequences. Contemp Account Res 14:533–566

Malik F (2003) Gefährliche Worte. Manag Mag 2003(12):98
Matschke MJ (1991) Finanzierung der Unternehmen. nwb, Herne
McKenzie CM (2004) Framing effects in inference tasks – and why they are normatively defensible. Mem Cogn 32(6):874–885
Mensch G (2002) Finanz-Controlling. In: Finanzplanung und -kontrolle. Oldenbourg, München
Meredith J (1988) Project monitoring for early termination. Proj Manag J 29:31–38
Meyer CA (2007) Working Capital and Enterprise Value. Gabler, Wiesbaden
Meyer MA, Vickers J (1997) Performance comparisons and dynamic incentives. J Polit Econ 105:547–581
Micklethwait J, Woolridge A (2003) The company. A short history of a revolutionary idea. Modern Library, London
Miller CC, Cardinal LB (1994) Strategic planning and firm performance: a synthesis of more than two decades of research. Acad Manag J 37:1649–1665
Mintzberg H (2009) Management. Berrett-Koehler, San Francisco
Müller-Stewens G, Lechner C (2011) Strategisches Management. Wie strategische Initiativen zum Wandel führen, 4th edn. Schäffer-Poeschel, Stuttgart
Nagel M, Mieke P (2014) BWL Methoden: Handbuch für Studium und Praxis. utb, Konstanz
Nevries P, Strauß E, Goretzki L (2009) Zentrale Gestaltungsgrößen der operativen Planung. Z Control Manag 53:237–241
o.V. WHU Controller-Panel. ▶ http://www.whu-on-controlling.com/zahlen/. Accessed 04 März 2017
Osterwalder A, Pigneur Y (2011) Business Model Generation. Campus, Frankfurt/New York
Pampel JR (2018) Digitale Horizonterweiterung – Begleitung der Innovation von Geschäftsmodellen durch das Controlling. Controlling 30(5):20–29
Petersen T (2020) Diginomics verstehen. Ökonomie im Licht der Digitalisieurng. utb, München
Reichmann T, Kißler M, Baumöl U (2017) Controlling with Key Figures, 9th edn. Vahlen, Munich
Roth A (2016) Introduction and Implementation of Industry 4.0. Basics, Project Management Model and Use Cases from Practice. Springer, Heidelberg
Sanders K, Kianty A (2006) Organizational Theories. VS, Wiesbaden
Schäffer U, Brückner u L (2019) Rollenspezifische Kompetenzprofile für das Controlling der Zukunft. Control Manag Rev 63(7):14–31
Schäffer U, Weber J (2015) Controlling-Trends & Benchmarks. WHU-Otto Beisheim School of Management, Vallendar
Schmalenbach E (1934) Cost accounting and pricing policy, 6th edn. Glöckler, Leipzig
Schmalenbach E (1962) Dynamic Balance Sheet, 13th edn. Westdeutscher Verlag, Cologne
Schreyögg G, Koch J (2010) Fundamentals of Management, 2nd edn. Springer, Wiesbaden
Schult E (1997) Financial Statement Analysis, Vol. 9. Edition S + W, Hamburg
Schweitzer M et al (2016) Systeme der Kosten- und Erlösrechnung, 11th edn. Vahlen, München
Seal W (2010) Managerial discourse and the link between theory and practice: from ROI to value based management. Manag Account Res 21:95–109
Silver D, Huang A, Maddison CJ, Guez A, Sifre L, van den Driessche G et al (2016) Mastering the game of go with deep neural networks and tree search. Nature 529:484–489
Simon H (1961) Administrative behavior, 2nd edn. Macmillan, New York
Simons R (1995) Control in an age of empowerment. Harv Bus Rev 73(2):80–88
Speckbacher G, Bischof J, Pfeiffer T (2003) A descriptive analysis on the implementation of balanced scorecards in German-speaking countries. Manag Account Res 14(4):361–387
Stadermann HJ (1987) Ökonomische Vernunft. Wirtschaftswissenschaftliche Erfahrung und Wirtschaftspolitik in der Geschichte. Mohr, Tübingen

Staw B, Fox F (1977) Escalation: the determinants to a chosen course of action. Hum Relat 30(5):431–450
Steinmann H, Schreyögg G (2005) Management, 6th edn. Gabler, Wiesbaden
Stocké V (2000) Framing und Rationalität: Die Bedeutung der Informationsdarstellung für das Entscheidungsverhalten. Oldenbourg, München
Stoffel K (1995) Controllership im internationalen Vergleich. Gabler, Wiesbaden
Sull DN (2005) Strategy as active waiting. Harv Bus Rev 83(9):120–132
Tengblad S (2006) Is there a new managerial work? A comparison with Henry Mintzbergs classic study 30 years later. J Manag Stud 43(7):1437–1461
Thaler RH (1985) Mental accounting and consumer choice. Mark Sci 4(3):199–214
Thaler RH (1999) Mental accounting matters. J Behav Decis Mak 12(3):183–206
Trapp R (2012) Convergence of accounting—a content analysis of the discussion of a approximation of internal and external accounting in German-speaking specialist journals. Gabler, Wiesbaden
Tversky A, Kahneman D (1981) The framing of decisions and the psychology of choice. Science 211(4481):453–458
Ulrich H, Probst GJB (1995) Anleitung zum ganzheitlichen Denken und Handeln: Ein Brevier für Führungskräfte, 4th edn. Haupt, Bern
Ulrich P, Stier J (2020) Veränderung des Rollenprofils von Controllern in Folge der Digitalisierung. Control Mag 45:10–15
Vanini U (2012) Risikomanagement. Grundlagen, Instrumente, Unternehmenspraxis. Schäffer-Poeschel, Stuttgart
Wall F (2001) Ursache-Wirkungsbeziehungen als ein zentraler Bestandteil der Balanced Scorecard Möglichkeiten und Grenzen ihrer Gewinnung. Controlling 13(2):65–74
WCED World Council of Economic Development (1987) Our common future. Oxford University Press, Oxford
Weber HK, Rogler S (2004) Bilanz sowie Gewinn- und Verlustrechnung, 5. Aufl. Betriebswirtschaftliches Rechnungswesen, vol 1. Vahlen, München
Weber J, Schäffer U (1999) Sicherstellung von Rationalität der Führung als Aufgabe des Controlling? DBW 59:731–747
Weber J, Schäffer U (2020) Introduction to Controlling, 16th edn. Schäffer-Poeschel, Stuttgart
Weber J, Bender M, Eitelwein O, Nevries P (2009) Learning from Private Equity Controllers. Wiley-VCH, Weinheim
Weitzmann ML (1976) The new soviet incentive model. Bell J Econ 7:251–257
Wild J (1974) Grundlagen der Unternehmensplanung. Rowohlt, Reinbek
Wild J (1982) Grundlagen der Unternehmensplanung, 4th edn. Rowohlt, Reinbek
Zünd A (1973) Kontrolle und Revision in der multinationalen Unternehmung. Haupt, Bern

GPSR Compliance

The European Union's (EU) General Product Safety Regulation (GPSR) is a set of rules that requires consumer products to be safe and our obligations to ensure this.

If you have any concerns about our products, you can contact us on ProductSafety@springernature.com

In case Publisher is established outside the EU, the EU authorized representative is:

Springer Nature Customer Service Center GmbH
Europaplatz 3
69115 Heidelberg, Germany

Batch number: 10726040

Printed by Printforce, the Netherlands